Inclusive Global Value Chains

DIRECTIONS IN DEVELOPMENT
Trade

Inclusive Global Value Chains

*Policy Options for Small and Medium
Enterprises and Low-Income Countries*

Ana Paula Cusolito, Raed Safadi, and Daria Taglioni

))OECD

WORLD BANK GROUP

A copublication of the World Bank Group and the Organisation for
Economic Co-operation and Development

Contents

Boxes

Figures

Tables

Foreword

Inclusive growth and the promotion of small and medium enterprises (SMEs) were two key priorities for Turkey's 2015 G20 presidency. Turkey called on the Organisation for Economic Co-operation and Development (OECD) and the World Bank Group to examine barriers that SMEs and firms in low-income countries face in enhancing their participation in global markets for goods, services, investment, and ideas.

The present report has been prepared in fulfillment of that mandate. It is the product of close collaboration between the two organizations, and draws upon the latest research.

SMEs are the backbone of all economies, developed and developing. In high-income countries, SMEs undertake the majority of private economic activity, accounting for more than 60 percent of employment and 50 percent of gross domestic product. In low-income countries, SMEs contribute significantly to broadening employment opportunities, social inclusion, and poverty reduction. In emerging economies, SMEs contribute on average more than 50 percent of employment and 40 percent of gross domestic product. However, despite their significance in most countries, SMEs are responsible for less than half of the value of direct gross exports.

A prominent feature of world trade during the last two decades is the rise of global value chains (GVCs), with goods and services being processed—and value being added in the multiple countries that are part of the chain. This has increased the interconnectedness of economies and led to a growing specialization in specific activities and stages in value chains, rather than in entire industries. Over 70 percent of global trade is in intermediate goods and services and in capital goods.

GVCs have thus provided an avenue through which countries can industrialize at a much earlier stage of development as producing firms choose to offshore fragments of the production value chain to countries where labor is cheaper or where other locational advantages confer a competitive cost advantage on the whole GVC.

GVCs are especially important for low-income countries where most firms are SMEs, for which the best metaphor would not be a chain but a ladder. The disaggregation of production into separate stages allows their firms not only to find their place on the ladder, but to move up the rungs as their capabilities improve. GVCs encourage that upward movement by rewarding skills, learning, and innovation. Overcoming obstacles to GVC participation can pay big dividends; developing economies with the fastest growing GVC participation have gross domestic product per capita growth rates 2 percent higher than the average.

The report finds that while participation in GVCs is heterogeneous and uneven, across and within countries, it is mostly taking place through indirect contribution to exports (backward links). The relatively low weight of SMEs in exports at the total economy level partly reflects compositional effects and associated economies of scale. Exporting SMEs are significantly underrepresented in (tangible) capital-intensive sectors, such as transport equipment, but compare favorably in the services sector, and also in heterogeneous sectors where specialization and branding can drive export penetration.

How can policy makers best respond to the reality of more interconnected economies characterized by the emergence of GVCs? What are the characteristics of a business environment that enables SMEs and firms in low-income countries to participate in GVCs, and facilitates upgrading opportunities over time?

This report offers answers to these questions. GVCs are the consequence of advances in information and communication technology and logistics, more open markets for trade and investment, and complementary policy frameworks that are appropriate for a country's stage of development. A key finding is that GVCs do not respond to piecemeal approaches to policy change. A "whole of the value chain" approach is needed. Some of these policies are horizontal in nature: good infrastructure and connectivity, a business-friendly environment, flexible labor markets and public investments in education and skills, and a range of other policies that improve supply chain capacity. Other policy initiatives are more targeted, such as removal of trade and investment restrictions, discriminatory subsidies, local-content or export-performance requirements, and restrictions on foreign exchange.

A better policy environment for more inclusive growth also requires investment in people, in skills, and in innovation—which are important drivers of GVCs. The highest proportion of value creation in a GVC is often found in certain upstream activities such as new concept development, research and development, or the manufacturing of key parts and components, as well as in certain downstream activities such as marketing, branding, or customer service. Such activities involve tacit, non codified knowledge in areas such as original design and the creation and management of cutting-edge technologies and complex systems, as well as management or organizational know-how.

Adequately coordinated trade and investment policies among nations are essential for GVCs to realize their full potential. While preferential trade agreements have become an increasingly important element of international cooperation, ensuring that they are coherent and complement the multilateral trading system under the World Trade Organization (WTO) remains a key policy challenge.

Multilateral action under the WTO is critical in helping to ensure that a wide range of countries and firms are able to benefit from opportunities for international specialization through GVCs.

Ken Ash
Director, Trade and Agriculture
  Directorate
Organisation for Economic Co-operation
  and Development

Anabel González
Senior Director, Trade and
  Competitiveness Global Practice
World Bank Group

Preface

This joint report of the Organisation for Economic Co-operation and Development (OECD) and the World Bank Group has been prepared at the request of Turkey's Presidency of the Group of Twenty (G20). It is part of larger multiyear work programs at the OECD and the World Bank Group, and it builds on earlier reports by the two organizations and other international institutions to successive G20 presidencies.

The focus of the report is on making global value chains (GVCs) more "inclusive" by overcoming participation constraints for small and medium enterprises (SMEs) and facilitating access for low-income countries. Two key facts emerge from this report: participation in GVCs is heterogeneous and uneven, across and within countries, and available data and survey-based evidence suggest that SME participation in GVCs is mostly taking place through indirect contribution to exports, rather than through exporting directly.

- *Heterogeneity in GVC participation.* Low-income countries are underrepresented in GVCs, although their integration has greatly expanded in the course of the past two decades: from 6 to about 11 percent of the world total. SMEs in low-income countries predominantly operate in the informal economy, and their participation in GVCs is concentrated in the agricultural sector and labor-intensive, very low value-added manufacturing and services activities, where entry costs are lower and not capital intensive. SMEs in middle- and high-income countries are operating in the low value-added end of the spectrum and in high-skilled and specialized niche activities. The increasing importance of knowledge-based capital within value chains, coupled with increased international fragmentation of these chains, has opened up new channels to integration through specialization in specific tasks.
- *Participation through indirect contribution to exports.* Most SMEs in high-income economies are very well plugged into GVCs as domestic suppliers of exporters. SMEs are vastly underrepresented in GVCs when looking at direct exports only.

The report makes the case that policy action, at the national and multilateral levels and through G20 leadership, can make a difference in achieving more inclusive GVCs through a holistic approach to reform spanning trade, investment, and domestic policies in G20 nations and in trade partner countries; also needed is investment in expanding the statistical basis and analysis of GVCs and in sharing knowledge on the best practices of enabling policies and programs. Three broad areas of recommendations are elaborated for consideration by the G20:

- To establish a trade and investment action plan for inclusiveness, defining clear and achievable objectives on trade and investment policy and identifying the necessary complementary domestic policy actions.
- To complement trade, investment, and domestic policy actions by providing the needed political leadership and support to enhanced collaboration across the public and private sectors and the establishment of global platforms for sharing best practices.
- To provide political support for the establishment of a realistic multiyear plan to expand and upgrade the statistical foundation necessary to increase the capacity of all countries so that they can identify and implement policies that will contribute to stronger, more inclusive, and sustainable growth and development globally.

Acknowledgments

This publication has been prepared jointly by the World Bank Group (WBG) and the Organisation for Economic Co-operation and Development (OECD). Ana Paula Cusolito (Senior Economist, Trade and Competitiveness Global Practice, WBG), Raed Safadi (Deputy Director, Trade and Agriculture Directorate, OECD), and Daria Taglioni (Lead Economist, Trade and Competitiveness Global Practice, WBG), are the main authors of this report. The authors wish to acknowledge the helpful contributions received for preparing the report, including from Nadim Ahmad, Head of Division, Statistics Directorate (OECD); Jean-François Arvis, Lead Economist, Trade and Competitiveness Global Practice (WBG); Christina Busch, Consultant, Trade and Competitiveness Global Practice (WBG); Michael Ferrantino, Lead Economist, Trade and Competitiveness Global Practice (WBG); Patrick Ibay, Consultant, Trade and Competitiveness Global Practice (WBG); and Dirk Pilat, Deputy Director, Directorate for Science, Technology & Innovation (OECD).

About the Authors

Ana Paula Cusolito is a Senior Economist specialized in innovation, productivity, entrepreneurship, and trade. She works in the Innovation and Entrepreneurship Unit of the Trade and Competitiveness Global Practice at the World Bank Group. She has conducted analytical and operational work on innovation, productivity, and international trade. She has experience working mainly in the Europe and Central Asia, Latin America, and Middle East and North Africa regions. Previously, she worked in the Central American and Integration and Trade departments at the Inter-American Development Bank.

Raed Safadi is Executive Director of the Research and Policy Directorate at Dubai's Department for Economic Development. He was the Deputy Director of Trade and Agriculture at the Organization for Economic Co-operation and Development in Paris, and worked at the World Bank in Washington, DC, and the Economic and Social Commission for Western Asia in Beirut. He has published widely on economic development and the multilateral trading system, regional trading arrangements, services, and environment.

Daria Taglioni is a Lead Economist and the Global Solutions Lead on Global Value Chains in the Trade and Competitiveness Global Practice of the World Bank Group. Ms. Taglioni's published work in economic policy analysis covers topics in international trade and finance, including firms' and countries' competitiveness in the global economy and the relationship between financial markets and performance. Before joining the World Bank Group, Ms. Taglioni worked at the European Central Bank and the OECD. She holds a PhD in international economics from the Graduate Institute Geneva.

Abbreviations

ABTC	APEC Business Travel Card
APEC	Asia-Pacific Economic Cooperation
B20	Business 20
BRICS	Brazil, the Russian Federation, India, China, and South Africa
CAGR	compound annual growth rate
CBTA	Cross-Border Transport Agreement
CIS	Community Innovation Survey
ECA	Europe and Central Asia
FDI	foreign direct investment
G20	Group of Twenty
GVCs	global value chains
ICT	information and communication technology
IFC	International Finance Corporation
IIRSA	Integration of Regional Infrastructure in South America
IPRs	intellectual property rights
ISIC	International Standard Industrial Classification
KBC	knowledge-based capital
LAC	Latin America and the Caribbean
LCRs	local content requirements
LPI	logistics performance index
MENA	Middle East and North Africa
MNEs	multinational enterprises
NTMs	nontariff measures
OECD	Organisation for Economic Co-operation and Development
PCG	partial credit guarantee
PV	photovoltaic
R&D	research and development
RTAs	regional trade agreements
SEZs	special economic zones

SMEs	small and medium enterprises
TFA	trade facilitation agreement
TiVA	trade in value added
UEMOA	West African Economic and Monetary Union
UNCTAD	United Nations Conference on Trade and Development
USDA	U.S. Department of Agriculture
USITC	U.S. International Trade Commission
WTO	World Trade Organization

Introduction

At the Brisbane Summit in November 2014, the Group of Twenty (G20) leaders concluded that trade and competition are powerful drivers of growth, increased living standards, and job creation. They also acknowledged that one important way for countries to connect to the global economy and develop is through global value chains (GVCs), a recognition that GVCs provide opportunities to empower the local economy with sophisticated imported technology, know-how, and a richer skill set. G20 leaders at the Brisbane Summit stated that "we need policies that take full advantage of global value chains and encourage greater participation and value addition by developing countries."

This report is part of larger, multi-year work programs by the Organisation for Economic Co-operation and Development (OECD) and the World Bank Group to support countries' policies on GVC integration with analysis and capacity building for leveraging GVCs for growth and development. The report builds on previous events and assessments promoted by the G20, including the G20 OECD-Turkish Presidency Stocktaking Seminar on GVCs (Paris, June 2, 2015) and reports by the two organizations and other international institutions to successive G20 presidencies on the implications of new measures of trade in value-added terms and the emergence of GVCs for trade, investment, and related policies.

The focus of the report is on making GVCs more "inclusive." Inclusiveness is defined in this report as overcoming participation constraints for small and medium enterprises (SMEs) and facilitating access for low-income countries. Emphasis is placed on the constraints to SMEs. The underlying assumption is that most firms in low-income countries are SMEs. And even larger firms in low-income countries are likely to face similar challenges as SMEs, including a less supportive domestic operating environment and weaker institutions that lead to higher fixed costs and challenges to competing in international markets. In discussing the challenges for SMEs, however, this report recognizes that important differences exist across world regions.

Two key facts emerge from this report. First, participation in GVCs is heterogeneous and uneven across and within countries. Second, the available data for OECD countries and survey-based evidence for low-income countries suggest that the participation of SMEs in GVCs is mostly taking place through indirect contribution to exports (backward links).

- *Heterogeneity in GVC participation.* The report finds that low-income countries are underrepresented in GVCs, although their integration has greatly expanded in the course of the past two decades: from US$259 billion in 1995 (or 6 percent of the world total of US$4.6 trillion), to about US$1.5 trillion in 2011 (or 11 percent of the world total of US$14 trillion), according to the OECD–World Trade Organization (WTO) Trade in Value Added (TiVA) database. Although SMEs in low-income countries predominantly operate in the informal economy, their participation in GVCs is challenging and is concentrated in the agricultural sector and labor-intensive, very low value-added manufacturing and services activities, where entry costs are lower and not intensive in tangible capital. By contrast, SMEs in middle- and high-income countries are operating in the low value-added end of the spectrum and in high-skilled and specialized niche activities. The increasing importance of knowledge-based capital in product value chains, coupled with increased international fragmentation of these chains, has opened up new channels to integration through specialization in specific tasks.
- *Participation through indirect contribution to exports.* The report finds that most SMEs are plugged into GVCs as domestic suppliers of exporters. SMEs are vastly underrepresented in GVCs when looking at direct exports only. However, in GVCs the indirect contribution to exports also matters. Survey analysis and case study evidence from the World Bank and new work at the OECD that links available national data on SMEs with the TiVA database show that the indirect contribution of SMEs is sizable in all OECD countries and significantly greater than what the value of direct exports would suggest.

The report makes the case that policy action, at the national and multilateral levels and through G20 leadership, can make a difference in achieving more inclusive GVCs. Two coherent sets of actions are proposed: a holistic approach to reform, spanning trade, investment, and domestic policies in G20 nations and trade partner countries; and investment in expanding the statistical basis and technical analysis of participation in GVCs and sharing knowledge on best practices on rules, policies, and programs.

Better Policy Environment for More Inclusive GVCs

G20 countries are the key trading partners for low-income countries, with around 70 percent of low-income countries' imports originating from G20 countries and close to 80 percent of low-income countries' exports directed to the G20. Thus, policy reforms that would lower trade costs in G20 economies and low-income countries can have important implications for GVC participation. GVC trade is particularly affected by trade barriers: when goods and services cross borders multiple times, as both imports and exports, trade costs are compounded. This is especially problematic for firms in low-income countries and for SMEs, which are less able to absorb these costs. Moreover, foreign direct investment (FDI) is the most common vehicle for countries to participate in GVCs. For example, the U.S. government estimates that intra-firm transactions constitute close to 50 percent of U.S. imports and around 30 percent of U.S. exports. According to the United Nations Conference on Trade and Development, an estimated 80 percent of global trade now occurs within international production networks of multinational companies. And it is these companies that are responsible for more than US$1 trillion in global FDI flows annually. FDI is vital for SMEs, as their natural predisposition is to join GVCs indirectly as upstream suppliers to exporters.

The G20 could lead progress in areas of trade and investment policy reforms that require collective action or that would benefit from individual policy actions by G20 members. For example, G20 countries could lead through their domestic growth strategies, leveraging on the fact that most lead firms in GVCs, turnkey suppliers, and global buyers are headquartered in G20 countries. Table O.1 provides a detailed list of trade and investment policy actions, distinguishing between national and collective G20 initiatives.

G20 governments, individually and collectively, have an important role to play in supporting domestic reforms at home and in partner countries. The domestic reform agenda is wide ranging, but priorities for the G20 and low-income countries include enhancing firms' productivity by building the internal capacities of firms and providing access to capital and connectivity, with particular attention to the needs of SMEs. A key requirement in this area is addressing issues related to informality. In low-income countries, many firms operate in the informal sector and choose to do so despite their growth potential. This is because the marginal benefits from increased production are often outweighed by the marginal increase in costs (regulatory and taxes) that are imposed by going formal. Removing potential barriers to growth and formality in the regulatory and tax framework is required, but incentives such as improved access to high-quality services, finance, and other requirements for GVC participation should also be used as channels for fostering formalization in low-income countries and partner G20 countries. Enhancing the productivity of firms requires removing regulatory and other barriers to the growth and scaling of SMEs, notably young and innovative SMEs. Doing so can help low-income countries to develop new areas of growth, and SMEs to reach a sufficient size to engage in international markets. For example, it would be helpful to promote the development of innovation ecosystems and move toward holistic approaches to evaluate creditworthiness that go beyond traditional balance sheet analysis.

The reform agenda will also need to focus on enhancing productivity through fostering the development of managerial skills and the adoption of better management practices, and through vocational training and lifelong education. Particular attention to information and communication technology (ICT) and broadband connectivity is needed, including access to and competition in ICT networks, as ICT-enabled business processes are central to participating in GVCs. Producing at world-class standards, as required by GVCs, means that quality

Table O.1 Priority Areas for Trade and Investment Policy

What: Establish a trade and investment action plan for inclusiveness, defining clear and achievable objectives on trade and investment policy, and identify the necessary complementary actions on the domestic agenda.

How the G20 can help: The G20 platform could address coordination failures between and within countries through a comprehensive action plan focusing on treating inward and outward trade and FDI in an integrated framework, giving as much consideration to imports and timeliness as to exports and market access. The platform could streamline import tariffs and simplify export procedures. The systems in place in the G20 finance track can be of guidance.

Items for consideration to be included in the trade and investment action plan for inclusiveness	National initiative	Collective action
Further the trade facilitation agenda by completing the ratification process of the WTO Trade Facilitation Agreement and by complementing improvements in hard and soft infrastructure and logistics services quality.	✓	
Better harness the challenges for SMEs to be competitive in GVCs, by relaxing policies such as rules of origin, and by agreeing to bring other policies, such as competition principles or standards, to the international level of policy; and through dedicated funding to aid for trade or through other capacity-building efforts supporting the preparedness of SMEs to comply with regulations.	✓	✓
Reform, nationally and in coordination with other G20 members, business services sectors in key network industries, such as logistics, supply chain management services, ICT-related services, e-commerce, and professional services, by removing barriers to entry and improving pro-competitive regulation.	✓	✓
Engage GVC lead firms, turnkey suppliers, global buyers, and SMEs in identifying binding constraints and solutions to investment attraction and promotion, for improving the investment climate and the absorptive capacity of SMEs, particularly in sectors known to generate strong upstream and downstream SME links, such as services, knowledge-based industries, and manufacturing sectors where specialization and branding are important.	✓	✓
Establish a G20 platform for identifying and implementing measures for the reduction of contractual frictions that act as a disincentive to the outsourcing and offshoring of valuable innovative assets. Prioritize minimizing transaction costs for SMEs (G20 micro-multinationals and investors and low-income country users of imported IP).	✓	
While developing and implementing rigorous IP legislation in G20 countries to protect innovative assets and attract foreign-owned technology, minimize transaction costs for SMEs by streamlining procedures and ensuring high-quality examination to increase IP signaling value.	✓	✓
Address the competition concerns of SMEs and low-income countries, regarding the behavior of large MNEs or anti-SME biases in the current functioning of supply chains, through establishing a dialogue on inclusiveness in GVCs with the B20.	✓	✓
Enhance cooperation and coordination between development partners at the multilateral, regional, and bilateral levels, with a view to making aid work better for trade, investment, and inclusive growth.	✓	✓

Jump-start the trade and investment action plan by a few concrete actions

- Establish a trade and investment action plan for inclusiveness.
- Commit to relaxing policies on rules of origin in G20 countries.
- Define "nuisance tariff level" and commit to the elimination of nuisance tariffs in G20 countries within a set timeline.
- Increase the focus of aid-for-trade and other programs in supporting the preparedness of SMEs to comply with trade and investment regulations.
- Establish a collaboration with the B20 to identify key binding constraints and solutions for fostering supplier diversity, focusing on efficiency of logistics services delivery and MNE-SME links.

Note: B20 = Business 20; FDI = foreign direct investment; G20 = Group of Twenty; GVCs = global value chains; ICT = information and communication technology; IP = intellectual property; MNEs = multinational enterprises; SMEs = small and medium enterprises; WTO = World Trade Organization.

certification and standards are increasingly important as determinants of competitiveness. Compliance with the many standards and technical regulations may be particularly burdensome for low-income country firms, and SMEs are often below the radar screen of consumers, so that the incentives to comply are lessened. Mutual recognition and convergence of dominant private and public standards would contribute to reducing these costs. Table O.2 summarizes the priority areas for capacity building.

Investment in Expanding the Statistical Basis and Technical Analysis of Participation in GVCs

A significant, and often overlooked, way to facilitate successful integration into GVCs, particularly for low-income countries, consists of identifying correctly the constraints, remedial actions, and efficacy of new policy measures. Country- and region-specific diagnostics, which also differentiate across firm types, are crucial

Table O.2 Priority Areas for Capacity Building

What: Complement trade, investment, and complementary domestic policy actions by providing the needed political leadership and support for collaboration across the public and private sectors and establishment of global platforms for sharing best practices.

Role for the G20: Help SMEs and low-income countries to develop new areas of growth and engage in international markets, a shared strategic vision, and greater collective action to target the major constraints. The G20 can offer the needed political leadership and clout with the private sector to leverage GVCs for a "race to the top" in participating countries.

Description	National initiative	Collective action
Informality Harness the growth potential of dynamic and innovative firms operating in the informal economy by removing the disincentives of going to the formal market, particularly for the informal businesses in the downstream parts of GVCs in low-income countries.	✓	✓
Policies for improving firms' productivity through learning, innovation, skill building, upgrading, and peer exchange		
Foster the development of managerial skills and the adoption of sound managerial practices, vocational training, and lifelong education.	✓	
Remove regulatory and other barriers to the growth and scaling of SMEs, notably young and innovative SMEs, including barriers to the entry, growth, and exit of firms.	✓	
Encourage collaboration with lead firms and global buyers to train local staff as a more efficient means of knowledge transfer and ensure that information is up to date and corresponds to the needs of lead firms.	✓	
Assist SMEs in the use of freely available technologies or the acquisition of technological licensing agreements.	✓	✓
Ensure that quality certification, technical regulations, standards, and conformity assessment procedures are nondiscriminatory and do not create unnecessary obstacles to trade; focus aid-for-trade programs on building capacity in low-income countries and for SMEs for the adoption of standards that lead to quality, productivity, and welfare upgrading; facilitate public and private sector preparedness for standards upgrading; promote convergence of public and private voluntary standards to reduce costs; and inform these processes through national and international guidelines.	✓	✓

table continues next page

Table O.2 Priority Areas for Capacity Building *(continued)*

Connectivity		
Support ICT and broadband connectivity. Strengthen broadband networks and improve access and competition. Foster services sector efficiency improvements and collective efforts to facilitate the access of SMEs and low-income countries to ICT networks.	✓	✓
Provide assistance to SMEs and firms in low-income countries, including through electronic platforms that help domestic firms acquire foreign technology and commercialize their IP.	✓	✓
Support physical connectivity and logistics. Assist countries in effectively implementing all aspects of logistics and transport sector reforms. Support capacity building to customize approaches to meet specific needs, operational circumstances, and national connectivity priorities.	✓	✓
Provide a continuum of potential support activities for ICT and physical connectivity, from infrastructure building to logistics and e-commerce performance assessments, to the development of practical implementation plans, to the identification of sources of financing for implementation plans.	✓	✓
Financing		
Enable finance that takes into account the intrinsic know-how, pool of talent, distribution channels, business relationships, business models, and access to technology in valuation of repayment ability.	✓	
Global platforms for capacity building		
Establish or support the scaling-up of global platforms for sharing best practices, learning, e-learning, and exchange. Foster private sector involvement on global platforms and use them for exchange of goods and services and cross-border financing solutions.	✓	✓
Provide a holistic, country-focused, multistakeholder approach to capacity building that is sustained over time, including engagement of the local and international private sector (local suppliers, global leads, buyers, and advanced consumers) and development partners, and creation of a private sector supplier base for advisory services on capacity building.	✓	✓
Concrete actions to jump-start domestic complementary measures to the trade and investment action plan		

- Establish collaboration with the B20 to identify key binding constraints and solutions for fostering supplier diversity, starting from addressing challenges in the areas of IP protection and technology transfer, quality, certification, standards, and efficiency of logistics services delivery.
- Support mature local, regional, and global facilities in the dissemination and scaling-up of best practices in the public and private sectors for sharing knowledge.
- Establish an action plan for universal ICT and broadband connectivity and empowering SMEs to leverage the digital economy.

Note: B20 = Business 20; G20 = Group of Twenty; GVCs = global value chains; ICT = information and communication technology; IP = intellectual property; SMEs = small and medium enterprises.

to guide policy. This cuts across the gamut of the statistical information system, including macro and micro (firm-level) data.

Recent statistical initiatives have improved understanding of GVCs, allowing estimation of trade flows in value-added terms. The OECD-WTO TiVA database is a well-known recent example of macro-level measurement and analysis of trade in value added. Although this database includes 61 economies, few low-income countries, especially in Africa and Central Asia, are included. Significant efforts are needed to develop and improve the national statistical building blocks that are required for inclusion in the TiVA database. Other standard macro-level data collection areas where further investment would be beneficial include Structural Business Statistics, Trade by Enterprise Characteristics, Entrepreneurship Indicators (Business Demography), and Foreign Affiliate Trade Statistics.

All of these standard collections require good data at the firm level. Investment in and scaling-up of micro data and existing data collections and surveys are therefore a central priority for better policy making. The World Bank Group's Enterprise Surveys use standard survey instruments to collect firm-level data on the business environment from business owners and top managers. The surveys account for firm size and cover a broad range of topics, including access to finance, corruption, infrastructure, crime, competition, labor, obstacles to growth, and performance measures, but not yet participation in GVCs. Other available data sets include microenterprise, informal, sector-specific, and other surveys, which could also be leveraged. Panel (longitudinal) data sets of survey results are available for many countries. These statistics constitute an excellent basis for expanding the available tools to document the better business relationships taking place in the context of GVCs. This includes collecting firm-level information on the links between exporters and foreign buyers, and between local firms and multinational companies integrated in GVCs (backward and forward links), as well as information on the internal and external factors facilitating or impeding the accession and upgrading of firms in GVCs. Table O.3 summarizes the priority areas for expanding the statistical basis and analytics.

Large and small firms exhibit different behaviors in the adoption of international certification practices and regulatory standards, and in the use of ICT and technology. These behaviors and the nature of participation in GVCs by firms in low-income countries are among the areas that can be better documented through embedding a GVC module in existing enterprise surveys. Impact evaluations of policies that can facilitate sustainable participation and upgrading in GVCs by SMEs and by firms in low-income countries are also necessary to strengthen the evidence base for policy making.

Table O.3 Priority Areas for Expanding the Statistical Basis and Analytics

What: Provide political support for the establishment of a realistic multi-year plan to expand and upgrade the statistical foundation necessary to increase the capacity of all countries to identify and implement policies that can contribute to stronger, more inclusive, and sustainable growth and development globally.

Why the G20 can help: The G20 is ideally placed to foster and support the generation of improved evidence-based analysis and policy advice, at the national and multilateral levels, through individual government action and relevant international and regional organizations.

Description	National initiative	Collective action
Investments in strengthening the micro-level data collection and analysis of firms in low-income countries and G20 countries, including by leveraging existing tools such as the World Bank Group's Enterprise Surveys and other World Bank Group surveys on microenterprises, the informal sector, and sector-specific and ad hoc surveys.	✓	✓
Improvement in the quality and availability of macro data in line with international standards, including input-output and supply-use tables for the OECD-WTO TiVA database as well as Structural Business Statistics, Foreign Affiliate Trade Statistics, Business Demography, and Trade by Enterprise Characteristics.	✓	✓
Impact evaluations of policy interventions at the firm level.	✓	✓

Note: G20 = Group of Twenty; OECD = Organisation for Economic Co-operation and Development; TiVA = Trade in Value Added; WTO = World Trade Organization.

CHAPTER 1

Setting the Scene

Introduction

Enhancing the integration into global markets of the goods, services, investment, and knowledge of small and medium enterprises (SMEs) is a policy priority for the Group of Twenty (G20) countries. It also represents a challenge for growth and job creation in all countries, at all levels of economic development.

Exports play an important role in fostering economic progress. Empirical research shows that firms that are connected to the global economy—through exports or foreign direct investment (FDI) or as suppliers to exporters—are generally more productive than firms that serve the domestic market only and typically rank among countries' most prosperous businesses. More productive firms, which are better equipped to compete in global markets, benefit from a virtuous circle that captures additional productivity gains through global value chains (GVCs). Higher productivity is also associated with higher wages and more prosperous communities. In countries for which data are available, workers in firms and sectors with high export intensity typically earn a substantial wage premium and show above average labor productivity. Similarly, there is a wage and productivity premium associated with FDI. By implication, communities connected to the global economy through large numbers of export-reliant firms, with inward and outward FDI, and with a strong domestic supplier base that serves exporters and FDI, are more likely to enjoy growing tax bases.

Imports also play an important role in achieving better economic performance, not only by making "world-class" inputs and capital goods available, but also by providing incentives for firms to innovate as they adopt knowledge, ideas, know-how, and best practices from abroad. Openness allows all countries the opportunity to absorb technologies developed elsewhere and grow at a faster rate. Investigation of the network of trade in value added reveals that being well integrated on the supply side is of paramount importance (Santoni and Taglioni 2015). Productivity growth relies on the diffusion of innovation from firms at the global frontier to other firms, which is facilitated by trade openness and participation in GVCs (OECD 2015). Far from being a handicap, a more open domestic market is a source of competitive strength, especially when complemented by a range of other policies to ensure sustained economic growth and diversification. For SMEs specifically, benefits also accrue in the form of exposure to international best practices, absorption of excess production capacity or output, improved resource utilization and productivity, and higher wages (Baldwin and Gu 2003).

A structural shift in the international division of labor has taken place with the rise of GVCs. The revolutions in information and communication technology (ICT) and transport, coupled with the development of ever more complex products, have allowed firms to establish chains that are geographically dispersed across the globe and as intricate as they are efficient (see box 1.1 for a discussion of the deep drivers of GVCs). GVCs have now become a driving force of global

---

Box 1.1 Understanding the Drivers of GVCs

Production systems today are very complex, with multi-layered international sourcing networks and fast-evolving, technology-enabled business models that increasingly allow cross-border economic activity to grow. The drivers are diverse; while some can be measured, others cannot.

The integration into the global economy of China, India, and the Russian Federation added huge product and labor markets that had been all outside the multilateral trading system before 1989, nearly doubling the field of play for internationalization (Freeman 2006). Faced with slow growth at home, large enterprises rushed to set up operations in those newly opened markets, especially in China, partly to carve out brand recognition and a market share in rapidly expanding consumer markets, and to cut costs on goods produced for export to international and home markets. For goods that require shorter supply lines, countries in Eastern Europe have joined traditional "export processing" locations, such as Mexico and North Africa. Moreover, under pressure from financial markets, large European and U.S. enterprises embarked on a "second unbundling" of corporate functions during the 1990s (Baldwin 2011). In an effort to focus on "core competencies," nearly every business function that was deemed "non-core" was subject to consideration for possible external sourcing from more specialized, more competitive, and often less unionized suppliers.[a]

Manufacturing functions were among the first to be externally sourced, but services followed very soon after. By the 2000s, the computerization of work and the emergence of low-cost international communication enabled a surprisingly wide range of services tasks to be standardized, fragmented, codified, modularized, and more readily sourced externally and cheaply transported across long distances. Even aspects of research and development fell under consideration for external sourcing. As in goods production, the application of information technology to the provision of services allowed some degree of customization within the rubric of automation and high-volume production, or what Pine (1999) calls "mass customization."

The rise of industrial capabilities in less developed countries created many more options for relocating work, and new players came onto the field. What previously had to be done within the confines of the multinational enterprise (MNE) could now be externally sourced

box continues next page

Box 1.1 Understanding the Drivers of GVCs *(continued)*

from newly competent suppliers and service providers with offices and factories around the world (Sturgeon and Lester 2004). The twin trends of external and international sourcing also meant that existing suppliers simultaneously received vast quantities of new work and were pressured to follow their customers to offshore locations (Humphrey 2003). At the same time and for the same reasons, the most efficient suppliers that were based in low-income countries grew rapidly from being small companies to becoming MNEs in their own right (Kawakami 2011). With the democratization of knowledge and accelerating technological progress becoming a mainstay of the global economy in the 21st century (Diamandis 2015), individual entrepreneurs can now start a company and take on functions that would have necessitated the complexity of a large MNE only 20 years ago. That is particularly the case for digital companies, such as Instagram, which has only 13 employees but a US$1 billion valuation.

As a result, the character of global production has changed. Large, brand-carrying MNEs, such as IBM, Siemens, and Toyota, nowadays rely on a complex web of suppliers, vendors, and service providers of all kinds and in multiple locations. At the same time, a set of highly influential global buyers gained scale and influence in the 1990s, including retailers such as Walmart and Tesco, and branded merchandisers such as Nike, Zara, and Uniqlo (Feenstra and Hamilton 2006). Building on successful experiments in the 1970s and 1980s by a handful of pioneering retailers, such as J. C. Penney and Sears, global buyers began placing huge orders with suppliers around the world without establishing any factories of their own (Gereffi 1999; Ponte and Gibbon 2005). Unlike traditional MNEs, where equity ties link headquarters with foreign affiliates, global buyers link to their suppliers through non-equity external sourcing ties. Often, intermediaries (for example, trading companies such as Hong Kong SAR, China's Li & Fung) are used to link buyers to producers in multiple countries.

Dicken (2011, 5) argues that the combination of those changes requires a different term: *globalization*, defined as "the functional integration of internationally dispersed activities." Today, GVCs combine the traditional drivers of internationalization (arm's length trade and intra-enterprise trade related to foreign direct investment) "with external international sourcing" that requires high levels of explicit coordination that differentiates it from arm's length trade (Gereffi, Humphrey, and Sturgeon 2005). In essence, external international sourcing arrangements imbue inter-enterprise trade with characteristics similar to intragroup trade: better control from the center, higher levels of bilateral information flow, tolerance of asset specificity, and harmonization and immediate integration of business processes that increase the potential for foreign activities to substitute for activities performed at home.

It is this last point, in particular, that underscores the opportunities for low-income countries and SMEs in such countries. Patterns of cross-border investment and trade based on product cycles—where producers from low-income countries receive older, outmoded products from high-income economies (Vernon 1966, 1979)—are rapidly giving way to more unified global production systems and markets, with different countries specializing in specific aspects, or stages, of the development and production of leading-edge goods and services.

a. See Sturgeon (2002) for a detailed case study of the trend toward external sourcing in the electronics industry.

economic growth. They have transformed the terms by which trade is conducted, and countries' patterns of industrialization. Rather than producing an entire product domestically, countries can now grow and thrive by specializing in specific tasks that allow them to integrate into parts of a value chain and reach a sufficiently large scale of production.

Policy needs to respond to the new reality by helping low-income countries to promote a business environment that not only makes their country an attractive location for those tasks, but also facilitates the creation of economic and social development from GVC participation. Addressing informality in the economy is a core requirement of GVC participation. The majority of firms in most developing countries are informal (Andrade, Bruhn, and McKenzie 2015; Bruhn and McKenzie 2014). Therefore, harnessing the growth potential of dynamic and innovative firms operating in the informal economy by removing the disincentives from going to the formal market, particularly for informal businesses that prevail in the downstream parts of GVCs and in low-income countries, is a precondition for making GVCs inclusive.

GVCs are especially important for firms in low-income countries. The unbundling of tasks and business functions typical of value chains increases opportunities to engage in global markets without having to develop complete products. It also unlocks access to (and so benefits from) knowledge and technology by learning from and interacting with other value chain actors in an integrated production process. Some of the opportunities from GVC participation have been seized, as testified by the increased expansion of GVCs in emerging and developing economies. GVCs encourage productivity growth by accelerating learning and innovation and by broadening and deepening the skill set in a country. Overcoming obstacles to GVC participation can pay big dividends if the appropriate supply-side policies are put in place. Developing economies with the fastest-growing GVC participation and pro-competitive policies aimed at addressing supply-side investment and trade expansion in an integrated manner have gross domestic product per capita growth rates 2 percent above average.

For policy makers, the question is not only how to connect to GVCs, but also how best to derive benefits from GVCs for the economy and society at large. Opening to international trade and investment is necessary but not sufficient to connect to GVCs and obtain the benefits in employment and income growth. Public and private investment to improve supply-side capabilities and the ability to exploit new market opportunities is also needed. Investment in people's education and skills is particularly important—and needs to be complemented with effective labor market policies and social safety nets to enable displaced workers to find new jobs. Moreover, strong framework conditions that are aimed at minimizing coordination costs and improving the legal and institutional environment for intellectual property rights and contract enforcement, proactive investment attraction policies, and emphasis on innovation and skills are also needed (Kowalski et al. 2015). For example, Costa Rica has gradually gained ground as a location for high-end manufacturing in small-scale, high value-added production (for example, medical devices). In short, successful participation in GVCs by SMEs and low-income countries requires a "whole of supply chain" approach that, internally to countries and internationally, moves away from the current silo approach of policy making. The approach needs to have different ministries involved in different parts of policy making relevant to GVCs, and to open up discussions—within governments and internationally—across the various policy areas that matter for value chain performance and that are seldom discussed holistically in international forums.

GVCs and Opportunities for Low-Income Countries

Many low-income countries are increasingly involved in GVCs upstream and downstream, and their participation brings about economic benefits in enhanced productivity, sophistication, and diversification of exports (Kowalski et al. 2015). High-income countries still exhibit, on average, higher participation rates, with European countries leading the way; but a clear trend has emerged, showing growing participation in GVCs beginning in the early 2000s, especially by low-income countries (figure 1.1). Economies in Central Asia, Europe, and Southeast Asia show the highest participation ratios, while countries in the Middle East and North Africa as well as Central America have lower but still important participation ratios. In contrast, many countries in the southern part of Latin America and in the Caribbean and South Asia, along with regions in Sub-Saharan Africa, trail behind. But even countries in these regions saw their participation grow considerably, notably between 2001 and 2011.

Cross-regional differences are significant in the way countries integrate into GVCs around the world (figure 1.1). Southeast Asia—the region where the most comprehensive and deepest regional integration agreements can be found—has the highest average share of intraregional GVC participation. In the other regions, the share of intraregional GVC participation is lower than that of extra-regional links. Still, East and Southern Africa and Latin America and the Caribbean show higher levels of regional integration than do Central and West Africa, the Middle East and North Africa, and South Asia.

But there is scope for much larger gains. The decomposition of gross exports by value added of the source country in the three headquarter economies of GVCs (Germany, Japan, and the United States) for selected sectors of importance (electronics, apparel and textiles, machinery, and transport equipment) provides an example of the potential gains that low-income countries can accrue through GVCs. Between 1995 and 2008, increasing value-added shares in these countries' exports originated in low-income countries. For example, the share of value added in U.S. exports of apparel and textiles increased from 3 to 8 percent. It increased from 2.8 to 5.1 percent in U.S. exports of electronics, from 2.7 to 5.9 percent in German exports of transport equipment, from 2.2 to 4.9 percent in German exports of machinery, from 2 to 7 percent in Japanese exports of transport equipment, and from 2.6 to 9.3 percent in Japanese exports of electronics (figure 1.2).

Figure 1.1 Average Total, Extraregional, and Intraregional GVC Participation across Regions, 2001 and 2011

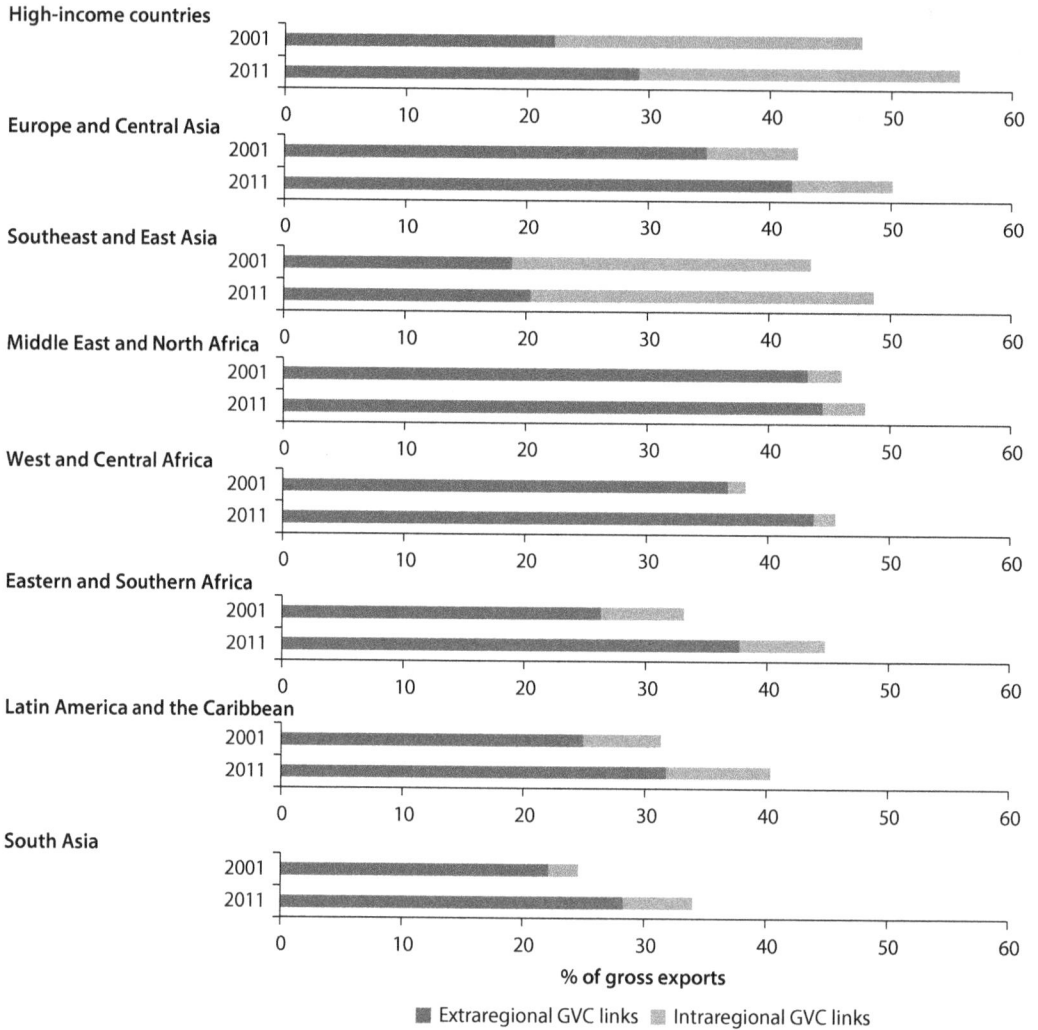

Extraregional GVC links   Intraregional GVC links

Source: Kowalski et al. 2015.
Note: These figures show the combined GVC participation ratio, which combines information about the use of foreign goods and services as inputs into a country's exports (backward participation) and where firms supply intermediate goods and services for other countries' export activities (forward participation). The ratio is expressed as a share of gross exports. GVC = global value chain.

GVCs not only shape relations between high-income countries and low-income countries, but also affect trade and investment ties between low-income countries. Emerging economies are now important sources of outward FDI. For example, the outward direct investment of firms in the BRICS (Brazil, the Russian Federation, India, China, and South Africa) rose from US$7 billion in 2000 to US$145 billion in 2012 and US$200 billion in 2013, which is almost one-third of global FDI (Gómez-Mera et al. 2015). Although most of those investors are driven primarily by market-seeking considerations (selling products

Figure 1.2 Domestic Value Added Embodied in Third Countries' Exports, Selected Countries, 1995 and 2008

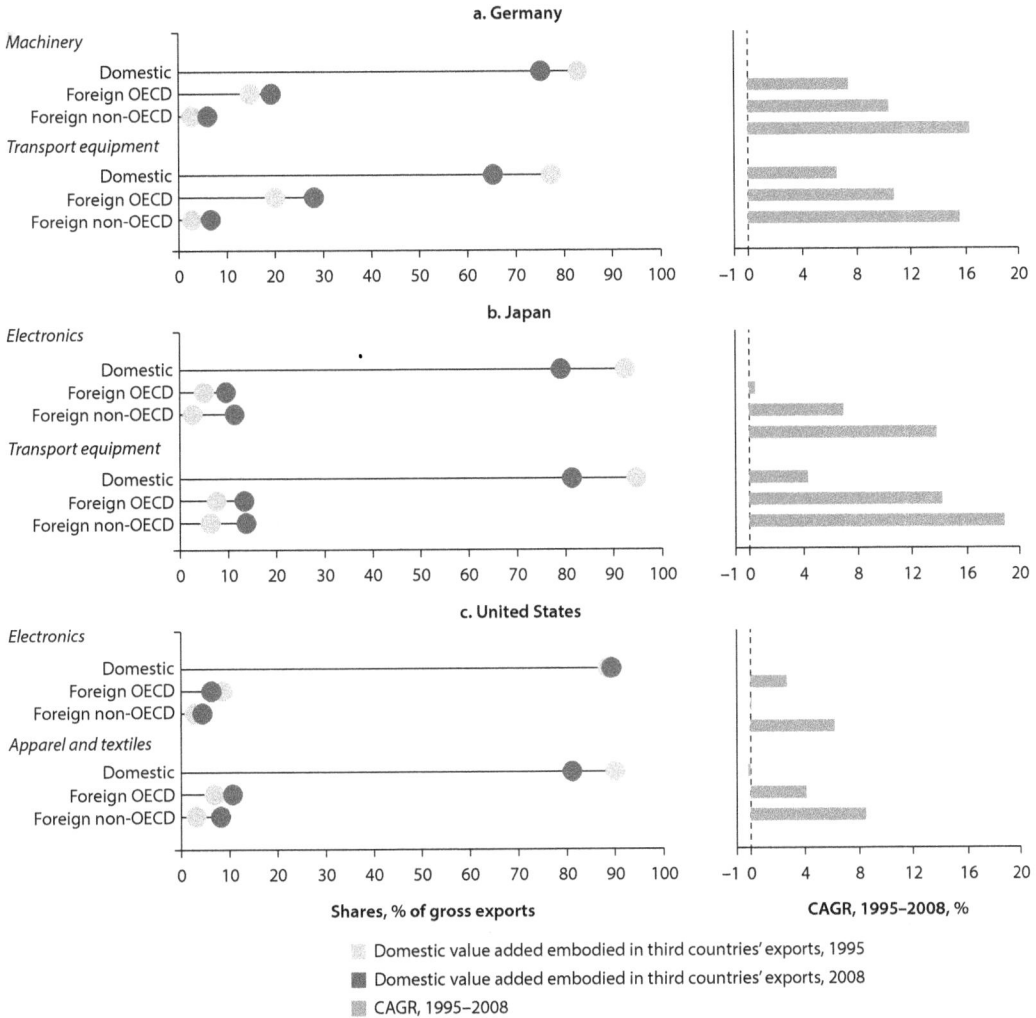

a. Germany

b. Japan

c. United States

Shares, % of gross exports

CAGR, 1995–2008, %

Domestic value added embodied in third countries' exports, 1995
Domestic value added embodied in third countries' exports, 2008
CAGR, 1995–2008

Source: World Bank computations using the Organisation for Economic Co-operation and Development–World Trade Organization Trade in Value Added database.
Note: CAGR = compound annual growth rate; OECD = Organisation for Economic Co-operation and Development.

locally), a subset is driven by lowering production costs. For example, the expansion of the Chinese apparel sector to lower-cost locations in Asia and the shifts of manufacturing activities within China are creating opportunities for learning in new territories. Some SMEs and firms in low-income countries have benefited from increasing participation in international production networks, others have increased the density of their production structure, and some have done both.

One of the more notable aspects of GVCs concerns their potential benefits for smaller providers at the firm and country levels. Whereas size mattered greatly in the traditional concept of trade and investment, which allowed firms to achieve economies of scale and tap into larger pools of skills and resources,

GVCs now offer an opportunity to overcome some of the inherent challenges associated with small size.

GVCs can offer less diversified and smaller economies new opportunities for finding their niches in the global economy. Market size still affects firms' decisions on where to base their manufacturing and service operations or their innovation centers, and the case for investing in a large market tends to be more compelling, yet small countries may overcome their size disadvantage. They can do so through the adoption of new policies, and opening their markets and linking them more closely to other, larger markets are likely to help. One of the principal draws for opening markets is that it allows producers in third countries to treat the smaller, connected country as an export platform.

Importance of SMEs

SMEs are the backbone of the economy in several developing countries. SMEs account for more than half of all formal employment worldwide (IFC 2013). A cross-country study of 49,370 firms in 104 countries finds that although SMEs (< 100 employees) have a comparable share of aggregate employment as large firms, small firms (< 20 employees) have the largest share of job creation and highest sales growth and employment growth (Ayyagari, Demirguc-Kunt, and Maksimovic 2014). These findings are also common in Organisation for Economic Co-operation and Development (OECD) countries, where 75 percent of new jobs are created by SMEs. Over the past several years, however, additional research has revamped the debate, indicating that size is not the relevant measure, but rather the age of the firm determines its contribution to net job creation. Evidence for Colombia (Eslava and Haltiwanger 2013), Morocco and Tunisia (Freund et al. 2014), and the United States (Haltiwanger, Jarmin, and Miranda 2013) shows that once firm age is controlled for, there is no systematic relationship between firm size and job creation, highlighting the role of start-ups and young firms in contributing to the creation of new jobs. But more evidence is needed to determine what kinds of firms play a significant role in net job creation in developing countries.

GVCs operate to the benefit of smaller firms, as they provide opportunities to specialize in tasks within the chain. Whereas SMEs would have found it difficult to compete along an entire line of activities, in the GVC world of today they can more readily participate in those tasks in which they have expertise, as long as the market failures that disproportionately affect SMEs are addressed.

Gereffi, Humphrey, and Sturgeon (2005) discuss in some detail the principal actors in GVCs and the power relations between them: MNEs, their affiliates abroad, and independent suppliers in domestic and foreign markets, including SMEs. Economic transactions within GVCs include intra-firm transactions between headquarters and affiliates, as well as transactions between companies and independent suppliers (arm's length trade and transactions accompanied by specifications on quality, product design, and so forth). The distribution of power and the direction of knowledge flows differ depending on the type of GVC.

They may be largely concentrated in the lead firm or MNE, or shared between lead firms and (upper-tier) suppliers. Factors such as the complexity of transactions, ability to codify transactions, and capabilities in the supply bases enter the equation (Gereffi, Humphrey, and Sturgeon 2005), but the business model's intrinsic characteristics matter too (Porter and Kramer 2011).

Owing to their size and capability to engage in international trade and investment, MNEs tend to be the leading actors in GVCs. MNEs organize global production processes across different geographical locations and through a complex network of affiliates (that is, offshoring), as well as through arm's length relationships with other companies and suppliers (that is, outsourcing). MNEs dominate exports. In fact, cross-border trade between MNEs and their affiliates—often referred to as intra-firm trade—now accounts for a large share of international trade in goods. And earlier firm-level evidence, based on gross exports data, reveals that exports are driven by a limited number of large, often multinational companies. For example, Mayer and Ottaviano (2007) show that 1, 5, and 10 percent of companies account for no less than 40, 70, and 80 percent, respectively, of aggregate exports in Europe. Similar results are reported for the United States (Bernard et al. 2007), as well as for low-income countries (Cebeci et al. 2012).

Although the evidence may show that GVCs are a "big-firm story" with MNEs as leading actors, those findings underestimate the importance and participation in GVCs of smaller firms, which often supply intermediates to exporting firms in their country and are, as such, integrated, indirectly, into GVCs. Slaughter (2013) finds that the typical U.S. MNE buys more than US$3 billion in inputs from more than 6,000 U.S. SMEs—or almost 25 percent of the total inputs purchased by those firms. Such domestic supplies are not reflected in international trade statistics, which count only direct exports; estimates for the United States show that in 2007 the export share of SMEs increased from approximately 28 percent (in gross exports) to 41 percent (in value-added exports) when such indirect exports are taken into account (USITC 2010). To quantify the direct and indirect participation of SMEs in GVCs across countries, chapter 2 of this report provides estimates of the importance of SMEs as upstream providers of the exporting sector. Unfortunately, such data are only available for OECD countries. Further investment in expanding the statistical evidence to cover low-income countries is warranted.

SMEs with high growth potential may grow over time to become lead firms in GVCs. Actors and links in GVCs may evolve as competitive (smaller) firms upgrade their activities and reinforce their positions. SMEs with high growth potential may seek new opportunities to expand their business abroad (OECD 2008), although it is generally difficult for them to reach international markets, with constraints being particularly strong in low-income countries (see, for example, Farole and Winkler 2014 for the case of Sub-Saharan Africa). Those SMEs whose competitive advantage is based primarily on cost or those specializing in certain types of services that require face-to-face interactions are more likely to participate in GVCs as domestic suppliers of the export sector.

Meanwhile, it is normally the SMEs at the forefront of technology or those producing high value-added parts and components that internationalize directly (Farole and Winkler 2014). The supply base of the automotive industry or the aerospace industry, for example, is double tiered, with large firms in the leading positions, but also including many small, specialized (and smaller) global suppliers (that is, second or even first tier suppliers) that often produce very specialized and customized parts and components. Often, as car assemblers set up final assembly plants in new locations, they provide support or urge their suppliers to move abroad with them (Van Biesebroeck and Sturgeon 2011). The fragmentation of production together with advances in ICT is also creating new entrepreneurial possibilities for SMEs to access markets abroad, giving rise to a new category of so-called micro-multinationals, which are small firms that develop global activities from their inception. The Internet and new business models make it possible for those smaller—often service-driven—companies to enter foreign markets at minimum costs (Mettler and Williams 2011).

GVCs hold promise for SMEs and firms in low-income countries if policy priorities include enabling firms' productivity growth through supporting their ability to build internal capacities and facilitating access to capital and connectivity. External international sourcing can lower barriers to exporting by accommodating specialization in narrow business functions, thus obviating the need for a company to develop a complex production process in-house and lessening its dependence on the degree of industrial development of the home country. Small labor force capabilities can be connected with complementary external capabilities, and small domestic markets can be connected with larger export markets. Those modes of integration share several requirements that allow relatively tight coordination and control.

At the same time, the existence of GVCs poses specific challenges for SMEs. First, the leading role played by large MNEs has led some to suggest that the emergence of GVCs might be a threat to the development of smaller firms in general. For example, the ability of smaller firms to capture value depends to a significant extent on power relationships in the chain, and power depends on several factors: for example, ownership of technology and the competitive situation in different segments of the chain. MNEs, which often have proprietary know-how and technology and a multitude of potential supply sources, might be in a strong position to dictate contractual conditions to their smaller suppliers. Still, MNEs, with their scale and access to markets and technology, may be the main channel for SMEs to participate in GVCs directly or indirectly.

Second, the fulfillment of strict requirements in product standards and quality as required by GVCs may be difficult for smaller and younger firms, and the market failures constraining their development differ from those faced by large firms. Smaller firms face specific difficulties that limit their growth, ranging from constrained access to credit and insufficient scale to support the costs of adequate research and development and training of personnel, to lack of lobbying power compared with larger firms and limited ability to diversify and absorb local and global shocks. Moreover, the smaller production scale of SMEs typically increases the recovery period of any fixed costs of investment or information acquisition, and the smaller pool of workers restricts the scope for reallocating the workforce efficiently across, or to new, tasks compared with larger firms. Young, innovative, and entrepreneurial SMEs may face additional problems, such as lack of access to risk capital or ill-adapted entry and exit regulations that prevent firms from experimenting with new technologies or business models (OECD 2015) and that can prevent them from reaching a sufficient scale to enter global markets.

All in all, the ability of SMEs and firms in low-income countries to be successful in GVCs (to adopt new technologies swiftly, learn by doing, innovate, and optimize their production) depends more heavily on framework conditions and externalities from the operating environment. Public goods and externalities that matter are wide ranging: from world-class logistics and ICT connectivity, to open markets, to the business environment, to the educational and vocational system, to the existence of a well-functioning innovation infrastructure and efficient forms of financing. Such challenges and how policy can address them are discussed in this volume.

The lack of a supporting environment can lead firms with high growth potential to long-term limitations not only for themselves, but also for the economy as a whole. Entrepreneurs may opt for suboptimal strategies that do not foster productivity and economic growth. These strategies include seeking loans from friends and family instead of formal sources of capital; limiting investment in technology that would boost productivity and growth; not hiring talent that can help the business grow and thrive over the long term; failing to adopt tools for identifying new market opportunities; and not seeking opportunities for scaling their companies, but instead putting the firms on a below-potential growth path.

Box 1.2 summarizes the take-away messages from this chapter.

Box 1.2 Key Take-Away Messages from Chapter 1

- Production systems today are complex, with multi-layered international sourcing networks and fast-evolving, technology-enabled business models, which increasingly allow cross-border economic activity to grow.
- Today's global value chains (GVCs) require high levels of explicit coordination that differentiates them from traditional arm's length trade. More unified global production systems and markets provide countries with greater opportunities to specialize in specific aspects, or stages, of the development and production of goods and services where comparative advantages exist.
- Rather than having to develop and manage the entire and complex production process in-house, GVCs offer opportunities to small and medium enterprises and firms in low-income countries. GVCs help in overcoming barriers to exporting by accommodating

box continues next page

Box 1.2 Key Take-Away Messages from Chapter 1 *(continued)*

specialization in narrow business functions and niche activities, and limit dependency on the degree of industrial development and the broader skills set in the country.

• Capitalizing on GVCs requires addressing informality in the economy and the right local business environment. The majority of firms in many low-income countries are informal and therefore excluded from GVC participation. Moreover, the lack of a supporting environment can lead to higher production and trade costs. This in turn can result in lower productivity and growth for the economy as a whole, as firms with high-growth potential adopt suboptimal expansion strategies.

• The challenges of producing at world-class standards as required by GVCs can be difficult to overcome for smaller and younger firms, and the market failures constraining their development are greater than those faced by large firms.

References

Andrade, Gustavo Henrique, Miriam Bruhn, and David McKenzie. 2015. "A Helping Hand or the Long Arm of Law? Experimental Evidence on What Governments Can Do to Formalize Firms." *World Bank Economic Review* 30 (1): 24–54.

Ayyagari, M., A. Demirguc-Kunt, and V. Maksimovic. 2014. "Who Creates Jobs in Developing Countries?" *Small Business Economics* 43: 75–99.

Baldwin, John, and Wulong Gu. 2003. "Export-Market Participation and Productivity Performance in Canadian Manufacturing." *Canadian Journal of Economics* 36 (3): 634–57.

Baldwin, Richard. 2011. "Trade and Industrialisation after Globalisation's Second Unbundling: How Building and Joining a Supply Chain Are Different and Why It Matters." NBER Working Paper 17716, National Bureau of Economic Research, Cambridge, MA.

Bernard Andrew B., J. Bradford Jensen, Stephen J. Redding, and Peter K. Schott. 2007. "Firms in International Trade." *Journal of Economic Perspectives* 21 (3): 105–30.

Bruhn, Miriam, and David McKenzie. 2014. "Entry Regulations and the Formalization of Microenterprises in Developing Countries." *World Bank Research Observer* 29 (2): 186–201.

Cebeci, Tolga, Ana M. Fernandes, Caroline Freund, and Martha Denisse Pierola. 2012. "Exporter Dynamics Database." Policy Research Working Paper 6229, World Bank, Washington, DC.

Diamandis, Peter. 2015. "You Can Manufacture What You Desire." *The WorldPost*, March 2.

Dicken, Peter. 2011. *Global Shift: Mapping the Changing Contours of the World Economy.* New York: Guilford Press.

Eslava, Marcela, John Haltiwanger, Adriana Kugler, and Maurice Kugler. 2013. "Trade and Market Selection: Evidence from Manufacturing Plants in Colombia," *Review of Economic Dynamics* 16 (1), pp. 135–58. Elsevier for the Society for Economic Dynamics.

Farole, Thomas, and Deborah Winkler. 2014. *Making Foreign Direct Investment Work for Sub-Saharan Africa.* Washington, DC: World Bank.

Feenstra, Robert, and Gary Hamilton. 2006. *Emergent Economies, Divergent Paths: Economic Organization and International Trade in South Korea and Taiwan*. Cambridge, U.K.: Cambridge University Press.

Freeman, Richard. 2006. "The Great Doubling: The Challenge of the New Global Economy." Usery Lecture, Georgia State University, Atlanta, GA. http://eml.berkeley.edu/~webfac/eichengreen/e183_sp07/great_doub.pdf.

Freund, Caroline, Bob Rijkers, Hassen Arrouri, and Antonio Nucifora. 2014. "Which Firms Create the Most Jobs in Developing Countries: Evidence from Tunisia." *Labour Economics* 31: 84–102.

Gereffi, Gary. 1999. "International Trade and Industrial Upgrading in the Apparel Commodity Chain." *Journal of International Economics* 48: 37–70.

Gereffi, Gary, John Humphrey, and Timothy Sturgeon. 2005. "The Governance of Global Value Chains." *Review of International Political Economy* 12 (1): 78–104.

Gómez-Mera, Laura, Thomas Kenyon, Yotam Margalit, Josó Guilherme Reis, and Gonzalo Varela. 2015. *New Voices in Investment: A Survey of Investors from Emerging Countries*. Washington, DC: World Bank.

Haltiwanger, J., R. Jarmin, and J. Miranda. 2013. "Who Creates Jobs? Small vs. Large vs. Young." *Review of Economics and Statistics* 95: 347–61.

Humphrey, John. 2003. "Globalization and Supply Chain Networks: The Auto Industry in Brazil and India." *Global Networks* 3 (2): 121–41.

IFC (International Finance Corporation). 2013. "IFC Jobs Study: Assessing Private Sector Contributions to Job Creation and Poverty Reduction." IFC, Washington, DC.

Kawakami, Momoko. 2011. "Inter-Firm Dynamics of Notebook PC Value Chains and the Rise of Taiwanese Original Design Manufacturing Firms." *The Dynamics of Local Learning in Global Value Chains: Experiences from East Asia*, edited by Momoko Kawakami and Timothy Sturgeon, chapter 1. Basingstoke, U.K.: Palgrave Macmillan.

Kowalski, Przemyslaw, Javier Lopez Gonzalez, Alexandros Ragoussis, and Cristian Ugarte. 2015. "Participation of Developing Countries in Global Value Chains: Implications for Trade and Trade-Related Policies." OECD Trade Policy Paper 179, OECD Publishing, Paris.

Mayer, Thierry, and Gianmarco Ottaviano. 2007. *The Happy Few: The Internationalisation of European Firms: New Facts Based on Firm-Level Evidence*. Brussels: Bruegel Blueprint Series.

Mettler, Ann, and Anthony Williams. 2011. "The Rise of the Micro-Multinational: How Freelancers and Technology-Savvy Start-Ups Are Driving Growth, Jobs and Innovation." Policy Brief, Lisbon Council, Brussels.

OECD (Organisation for Economic Co-operation and Development). 2008. *Enhancing the Role of SMEs in Global Value Chains*. Paris: OECD Publishing.

———. 2015. *OECD Innovation Strategy 2015: An Agenda for Policy Action*. Paris: OECD Publishing.

Pine, B. Joseph II. 1999. *Mass Customization: The New Frontier in Business Competition*. Cambridge, MA: Harvard Business School Press.

Ponte, Stefano, and Peter Gibbon. 2005. "Quality Standards, Conventions and the Governance of Global Value Chains." *Economy and Society* 34 (1): 1–31.

Porter, Michael, and Mark Kramer. 2011. "Creating Shared Value." *Harvard Business Review* 89 (1/2): 62–77.

Santoni, Gianluca, and Daria Taglioni. 2015. "Networks and Structural Integration in Global Value Chains." In *The Age of Global Value Chains*, edited by João Amador and Filippo di Mauro. Washington, DC: Center for Economic Policy Research.

Slaughter, Matthew J. 2013. "American Companies and Global Supply Networks: Driving U.S. Economic Growth and Jobs by Connecting the World." U.S. Council for International Business and the United States Council Foundation, New York.

Sturgeon, Timothy. 2002. "Modular Production Networks. A New American Model of Industrial Organization." *Industrial and Corporate Change* 11 (3): 451–96.

Sturgeon, Timothy, and Richard K. Lester. 2004. "The New Global Supply-Base: New Challenges for Global Suppliers in East Asia." *Global Production Networking and Technological Change in East Asia*, edited by Shahid Yusuf, M. Anjum Altaf, and Kaoru Nabeshima. Washington, DC: World Bank.

USITC (United States International Trade Commission). 2010. *Small and Medium-Sized Enterprises: Characteristics and Performance*. USITC Publication 4189, Washington, DC.

Van Biesebroeck, Johannes, and Timothy J. Sturgeon. 2011. "Global Value Chains in the Automotive Industry: An Enhanced Role for Developing Countries?" *International Journal of Technological Learning, Innovation and Development* 4 (1/2/3): 181–205.

Vernon, Raymond. 1966. "International Investment and International Trade in the Product Cycle." *Quarterly Journal of Economics* 80 (2): 190–207.

Vernon, Raymond. 1979. "The Product Cycle Hypothesis in the New International Environment." *Oxford Bulletin of Economic and Statistics* 41, 255–267.

CHAPTER 2

Stylized Facts on SMEs in GVCs

Informality of the Economy: A Binding Constraint

Global value chains (GVCs) operate in the formal market. Yet, the majority of firms in many developing countries are informal (Andrade, Bruhn, and McKenzie 2015; Bruhn and McKenzie 2014). In Sri Lanka, for example, only one-fifth of firms operating without paid workers are registered with any government agency. Even among firms employing paid workers, the majority are unregistered with one or more pertinent agencies (de Mel, McKenzie, and Woodruff 2013). According to International Labour Organization surveys in 47 developing economies, the share of persons in informal employment is above 50 percent in several countries, including the Arab Republic of Egypt, Bolivia, Colombia, Ecuador, El Salvador, Honduras, India, Indonesia, Liberia, Madagascar, Mali, and Mexico.

Although more analysis is needed, World Bank assessments from the institution's Independent Evaluation Group indicate that about 32 percent of the firms with 10–99 employees in a sample of developing countries report informality as one of the top five constraints they face in doing business. Other constraints for this class of firms are power, corruption, the tax rate, and political instability. By way of comparison, for the largest firms (300+ employees), the top constraints are power, worker skills, transportation, the tax rate, and corruption.

Participation in GVCs: Direct Insertion

Firms in the formal economy can join GVCs by directly participating in exports (of goods and services that feed into third countries' production) or by indirectly supplying other exporters, such as large local firms or multinational companies.

Small and medium enterprises (SMEs) are typically less export oriented than are large firms. In Organisation for Economic Co-operation and Development (OECD) countries for which data on export participation by firm size are available, SMEs (firms with fewer than 250 employees) represent the vast majority of the business population (table 2.1). They also account for the majority of employment in all OECD countries.

Table 2.1 Percentage of Exporters, by Number of Employees and Foreign Ownership, Mining and Quarrying, Manufacturing, Electricity, Gas, Steam and Air Conditioning Supply, and Water Supply, Sewerage, Waste Management, and Remediation Activities (ISIC rev. 4 - sectors 5–39), 2011

Country	All firms	Firms, by number of employees				Foreign-controlled
		0–9	10–49	50–249	250+	
Austria	31	19	56	90	97	86
Belgium	24	15	62	84	96	97
Bulgaria	18	7	38	72	77	—
Canada	28	14	44	91	100	—
Germany	24	17	28	51	52	36
Denmark	30	19	55	83	100	91
Spain	12	6	37	76	86	75
Estonia	42	31	69	79	79	100
Finland	18	11	44	72	89	81
France	12	5	45	83	100	80
Hungary	20	11	63	80	87	78
Italy	20	12	53	84	87	71
Lithuania	21	8	61	81	86	—
Luxembourg	45	27	71	91	100	—
Latvia	31	18	66	83	84	—
Poland	14	8	48	65	87	100
Portugal	19	11	53	82	89	57
Romania	15	5	27	63	81	—
Slovak Republic	9	4	63	99	100	100
Slovenia	25	19	68	78	90	—
Sweden	19	12	65	80	88	78
United Kingdom	24	14	48	72	77	58
United States	9	5	16	51	53	—

Sources: OECD/Eurostat Trade by Enterprise Characteristics database; OECD Structural and Demographic Business Statistics database; OECD Activity of Multinational Enterprises database.
Note: ISIC = International Standard Industrial Classification; OECD = Organisation for Economic Co-operation and Development. — = not available.

However, despite their significance, SMEs are responsible in most countries for less than half of the value of gross exports (figure 2.1). For example, they account for less than 10 percent of gross manufacturing exports in Mexico. The share of SMEs in exports is larger in small, open economies, such as Estonia, Ireland, and Latvia, and in countries where SME firms have traditionally dominated the business landscape, such as Italy. But on the whole, large firms dominate, thus reflecting their greater outward orientation (figure 2.2). Most large manufacturing firms engage in direct exports, but the percentage of direct exporters among SMEs is systematically lower across countries and industries, with microenterprises in particular rarely exporting directly.

In most countries, only a small proportion of firms (almost exclusively large) account for a disproportionate share of overall exports (figure 2.3).

Figure 2.1 Contribution of SMEs to Gross Manufacturing Direct Exports, 2012

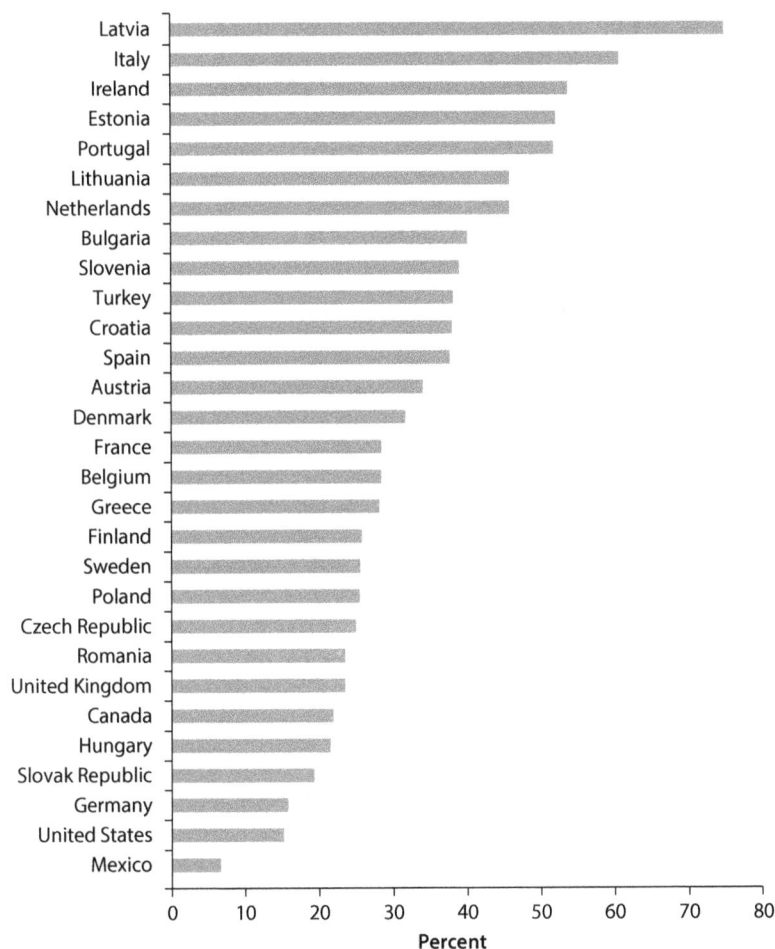

Sources: OECD/Eurostat Trade by Enterprise Characteristics database; OECD Structural and Demographic Business Statistics database.
Note: OECD = Organisation for Economic Co-operation and Development; SMEs = small and medium enterprises.

This finding is in line with much of the firm-level evidence on export activity from countries worldwide. In most industries, a few large firms account for extremely large shares of output and employment. For example, Mayer and Ottaviano (2007) show that 1, 5, and 10 percent of companies account for no less than 40, 70, and 80 percent, respectively, of Europe's aggregate exports. Cebeci et al. (2012) and subsequent research based on the World Bank Exporter Dynamics Database (which provides measures of exporter character-istics and dynamics across 70 countries of all income levels and geographic regions) confirm that similar trends hold for low-income countries. They find that the top 5 percent of firms accounts on average for 80 percent of exports.

The relatively low weight of SMEs in exports at the total economy level partly reflects compositional effects. Exporting SMEs are significantly

Figure 2.2 Export Intensities: Exports-to-Turnover Ratios, 2012

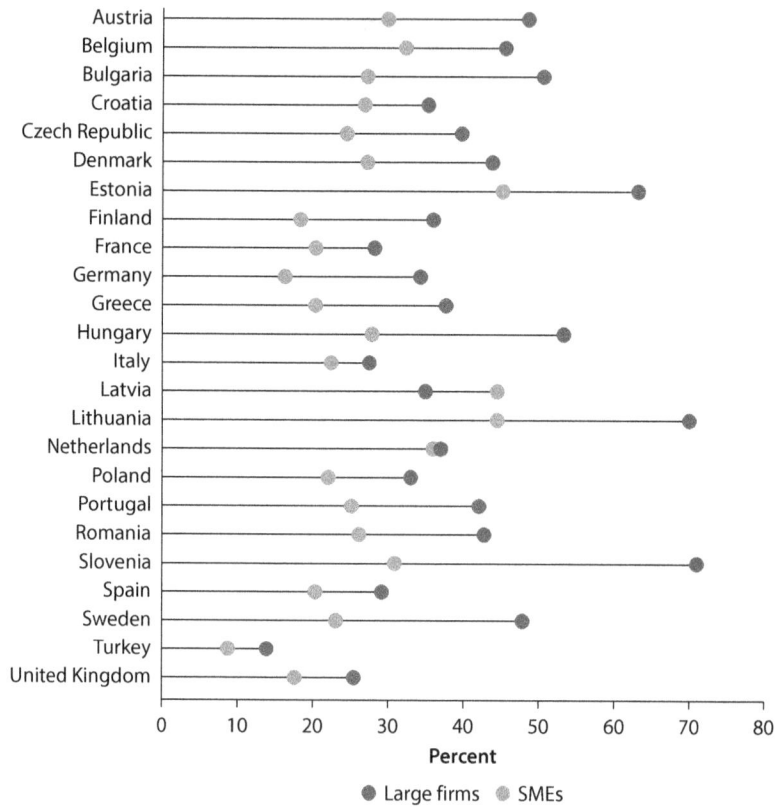

Source: OECD 2015.
Note: OECD = Organisation for Economic Co-operation and Development; SMEs = small and medium enterprises.

underrepresented in (tangible) capital-intensive sectors, such as transport equipment, but they compare favorably in the services sector (figure 2.4, panels a, b, c, d), where the fixed costs of entry are presumably lower. The same holds for heterogeneous manufacturing sectors where specialization and branding may drive export penetration (figure 2.4, panels e, f, g).

The data also reveal a correlation between firm size and presence in more distant markets. For example, in 2011, European SMEs accounted for 37 percent of intra–European Union exports, but only 28 percent of extra–European Union exports. In line with the findings from the literature on firm heterogeneity (Bernard, Jensen, and Schott 2003), compared with larger firms, SMEs in most countries typically export disproportionately more to neighboring countries.

Figure 2.5 illustrates that for most countries, where data are available, this finding holds. In Mexico, where "extraregional" reflects exports to the world, excluding the United States, the data show that SMEs typically have a higher share of their direct exports going to the rest of the world than to the United States. This fact may reflect, in part, the significant processing *maquiladora*

Figure 2.3 Share of Top Exporters in Total Export Values, 2012

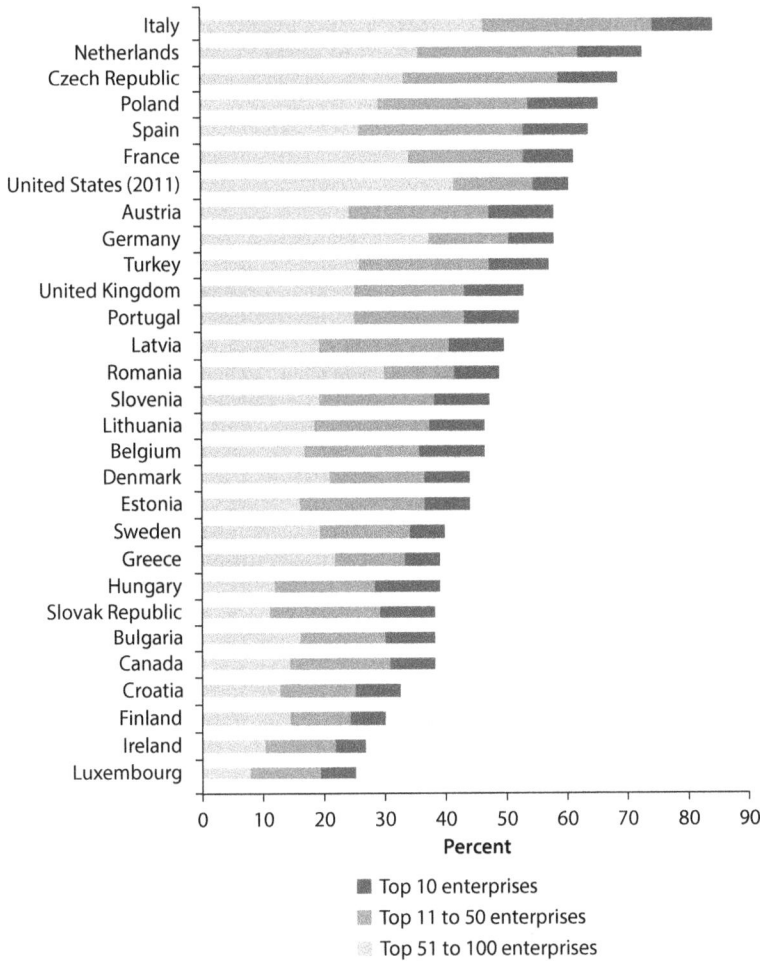

Top 10 enterprises
Top 11 to 50 enterprises
Top 51 to 100 enterprises

Source: OECD 2015.

relationships developed with U.S. firms. In many Eastern European economies, the share of exports outside the European Union is particularly small for large and small firms. The structure of European GVCs, whereby Germany plays the role of hub for final goods, may be at the origin of those results. Small firms in Germany have managed to diversify their export markets (exporting outside the European Union) to a greater extent than have many large enterprises in other European economies, thereby confirming the strength of the German *mittelstand* and possibly a very effective business supporting environment.

Although participation in exports is lower for SMEs, opportunities exist to exploit high value-added niches in GVCs, particularly in market segments in which input costs are low. One such case is organic agricultural production (Staritz and Reis 2013). An industry that began retailing in the 1980s and that is driven by high demand, it also receives high premiums over conventionally

Figure 2.4 Share of Gross Direct Export Value by SMEs, 2012

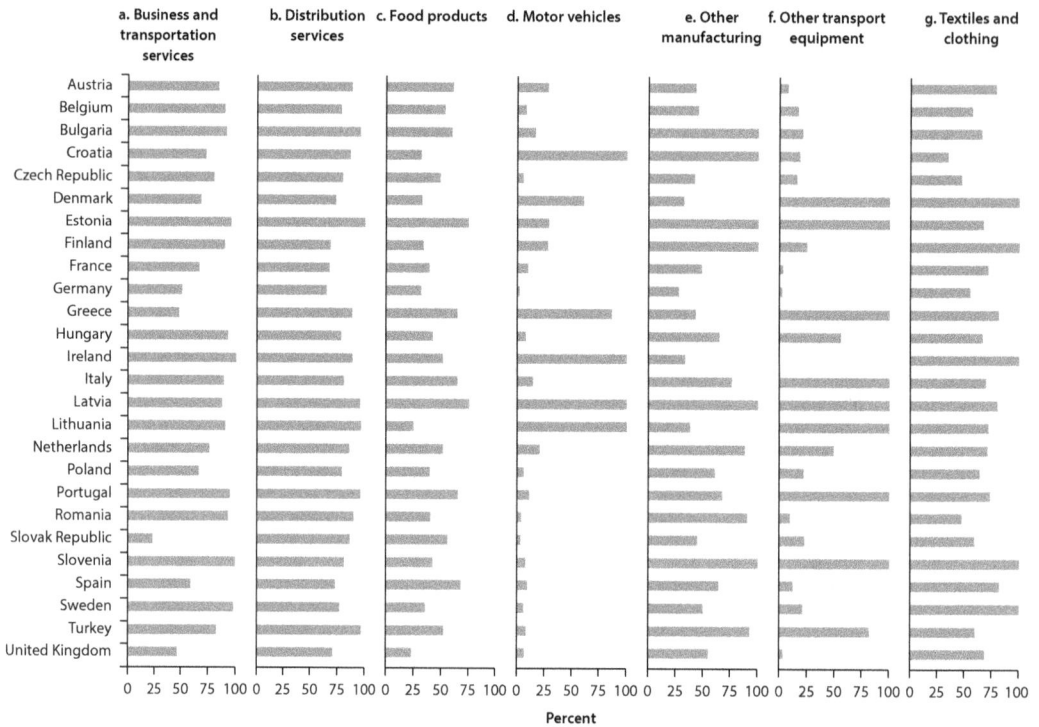

Source: OECD/Eurostat Trade by Enterprise Characteristics database.
Note: OECD = Organisation for Economic Co-operation and Development; SMEs = small and medium enterprises.

produced crops. For example, organic blueberries earn a premium of more than 100 percent (USDA 2011a,b). A study by Farnworth and Hutchings (2009) that surveyed organic production in Bangladesh found that firms in this segment had (a) greater decision power over buyers, (b) improved positions within the value chain, and (c) greater access to inputs and markets for organic products than for traditional products. The fact that those staples do not use pesticides decreases key input costs, and the fact that they are produced in small plots reduces the constraints from scale. A case study of female-owned Ugandan SMEs that export organic fruits and vegetables further reveals the significant premiums paid for organic products. The access to low-cost capital provides opportunities for product and process upgrading, as well as increased productivity.

Moreover, statistical evidence shows that some SMEs outperform large firms (in the share of their output destined for export markets) in some market segments, partly reflecting their involvement in tasks at the higher end of the value chain—such as research and development, design, and branding—that drive higher relative labor productivity. Case study literature indicates that SMEs may be more agile than large firms in inter-sector upgrading, whereas start-ups (which tend to be SMEs) may contribute substantially not only to innovation, but also to employees' training in innovative sectors.

Figure 2.5 Share of Gross Direct Export Value of Small and Large Firms by Destination, 2009

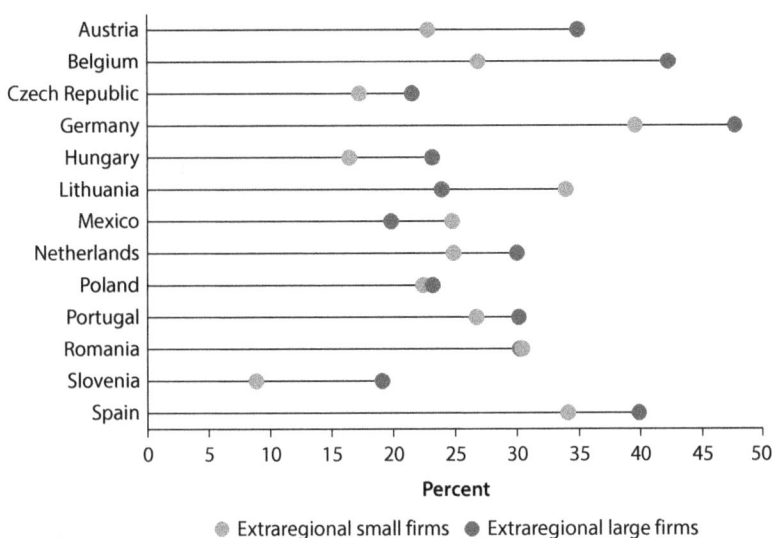

Source: OECD/Eurostat Trade by Enterprise Characteristics database.

Data for OECD countries in the "other manufacturing" sector, for example, reveal that the average export intensity of a country's SMEs is high when average productivity is low or high (figure 2.6), thus illustrating the scope for integration through high value-added niches in GVCs and not just through cost-saving models.

Suppliers of Large Local and Multinational Firms: Indirect Insertion

The findings on direct participation underestimate the participation in GVCs of smaller firms, which often supply intermediates to exporting firms in their country and are, as such, relatively more integrated in domestic value chains. Slaughter (2013) calculates that the typical U.S. multinational enterprise (MNE) buys more than US$3 billion in inputs from more than 6,000 SMEs in the United States—or almost 25 percent of the total input purchased by those firms. Those domestic supplies are not reflected in international trade statistics, which count only direct exports. Estimates for the United States show that in 2007 the export share of SMEs increased from approximately 28 percent (in gross exports) to 41 percent (in value-added exports), when such indirect exports are taken into account (USITC 2010).

Exploratory work links national data on SMEs within the Inter-Country Input-Output tables developed for the OECD–World Trade Organization Trade in Value Added initiative. It shows that the indirect contribution of SMEs is several times greater than the direct participation in all countries for which data were available. Accounting for the contribution that SMEs make to exports as upstream producers, in the majority of cases, SMEs account for more than half of the total exports of domestic value added (trade in value added) (figure 2.7). The effect of including

Figure 2.6 Export Intensity and Labor Productivity

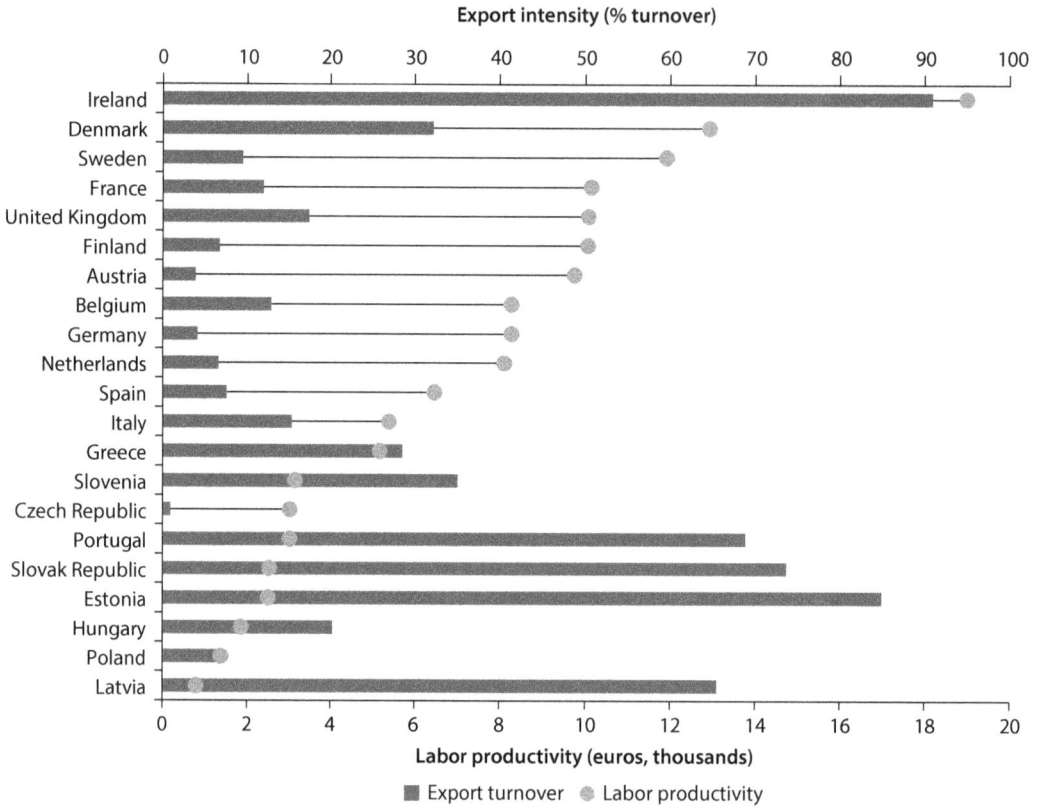

Source: Organisation for Economic Co-operation and Development/Eurostat Trade by Enterprise Characteristics database.

the contribution of upstream SME suppliers is particularly large in countries such as Mexico, where the share of SMEs in direct value-added exports is lower. At the total economy level, for example, the contribution of SMEs nearly doubles, from around 16 to about 33 percent of total exports of domestic value added.

But despite greater integration within countries, significant differences remain across countries in the scale of integration, a picture that is reinforced by specific sectors. For example, the contribution of SMEs to total exports of manufactured goods remained relatively low in 2009 in Hungary and Mexico, even after including upstream inputs (from manufacturing and services SME upstream suppliers) (figure 2.8). With relatively high foreign ownership (directly through foreign investment or indirectly through operational control of production chains) in Hungary and Mexico, the relatively low contribution of SMEs (coupled with the relatively high foreign content of exports) points to principal "controlling" firms that use foreign upstream suppliers, resulting in fewer spillovers to the SME sector. This finding suggests that improved upstream integration in both countries could be achieved through upgrading the SME population to meet the quality standards, requirements, and specifications of the exporting (larger) firms. But more broadly,

Figure 2.7 Share of SMEs in Exports: Total Economy, 2009

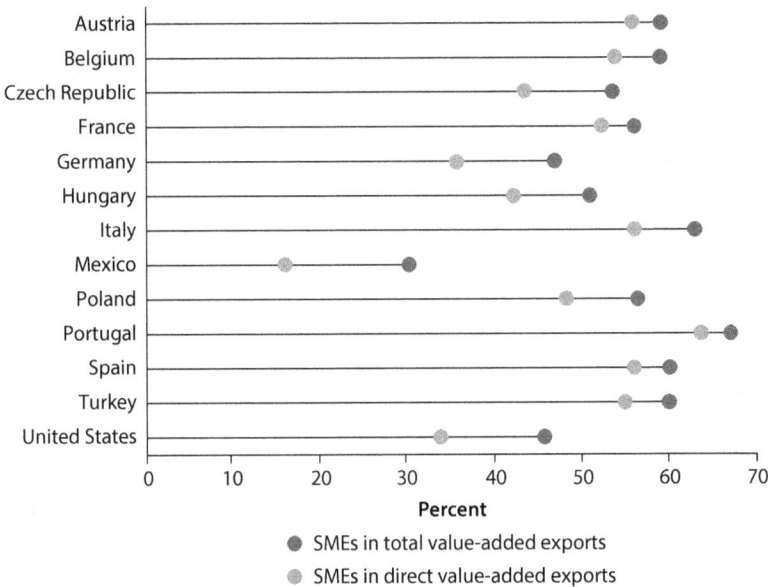

Sources: OECD/Eurostat Trade by Enterprise Characteristics database; OECD Structural and Demographic Business Statistics database; OECD Intercountry Input-Output Trade in the Value Added database.
Note: OECD = Organisation for Economic Co-operation and Development; SMEs = small and medium enterprises.

it may also require consideration of the informal sector, especially because self-employment rates are around one-quarter of the workforce in Mexico.

SMEs tend to channel their value added for exports through large firms rather than through other SMEs (figure 2.9). Integration of SMEs through larger enterprises within GVCs varies across countries, but it is significant in all cases, thereby representing over half of total exports of value added by SMEs in the Czech Republic, France, Germany, Italy, Mexico, and Poland; the case of Mexico largely reflects the relatively low direct exports of SMEs.

It is noteworthy that even in those sectors where the direct contribution of SMEs may be marginal (for example, the motor vehicles sector), the contribution of SMEs to total domestic value added that is embodied in exports can be significant from the upstream material input suppliers and upstream SME services suppliers (figure 2.10).

In many OECD countries, SMEs are the main exporters of business services. Including the upstream contribution made by other SMEs reinforces their significance (figure 2.11). In 2009, for example, one-third of the total domestic value-added content of exports in the business services sector in the United States originated in direct exports by business services SMEs. But when the upstream inputs in other service (distribution) sectors and upstream manufacturers are included, the overall contribution of SMEs to domestic value added that is embodied in service exports was greater than half.

Figure 2.8 Share of SMEs in Exports: Manufacturing, 2009

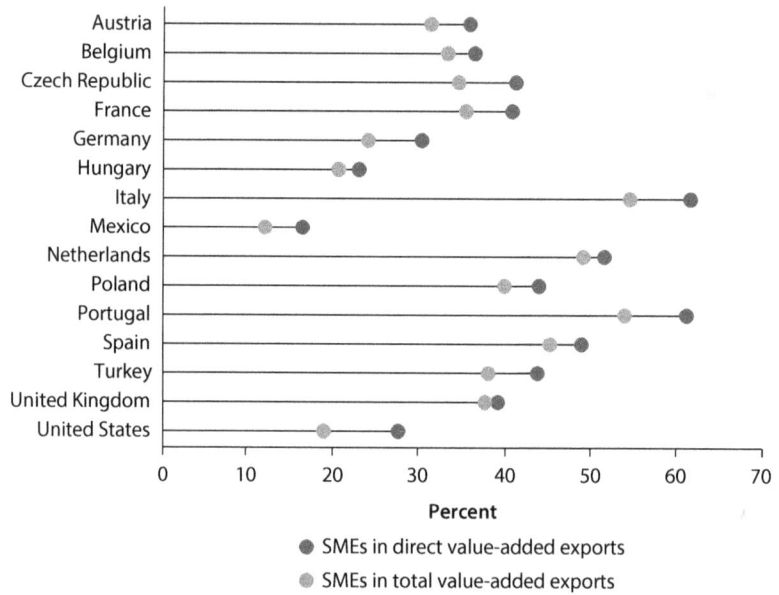

Sources: OECD/Eurostat Trade by Enterprise Characteristics database; OECD Structural and Demographic
Business Statistics database; OECD Intercountry Input-Output Trade in the Value Added database.
Note: OECD = Organisation for Economic Co-operation and Development; SMEs = small and medium
enterprises.

**Figure 2.9 Upstream Exports of SMEs through Large Firms, Share of Total
Exports of Value Added by SMEs: Whole Economy, 2009**

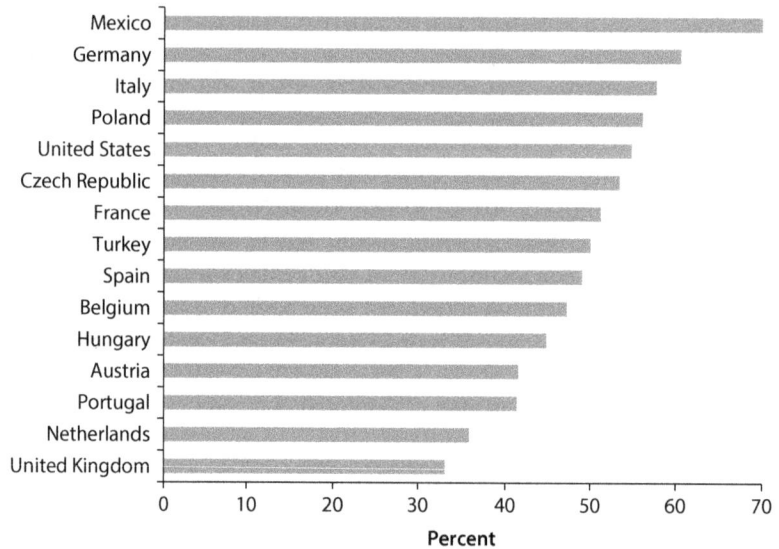

Sources: OECD/Eurostat Trade by Enterprise Characteristics database; OECD Structural and Demographic
Business Statistics database; OECD Intercountry Input-Output Trade in the Value Added database.
Note: OECD = Organisation for Economic Co-operation and Development; SMEs = small and medium
enterprises.

Figure 2.10 SME Share of Total Domestic Value Added of Exports of Motor Vehicles, 2009

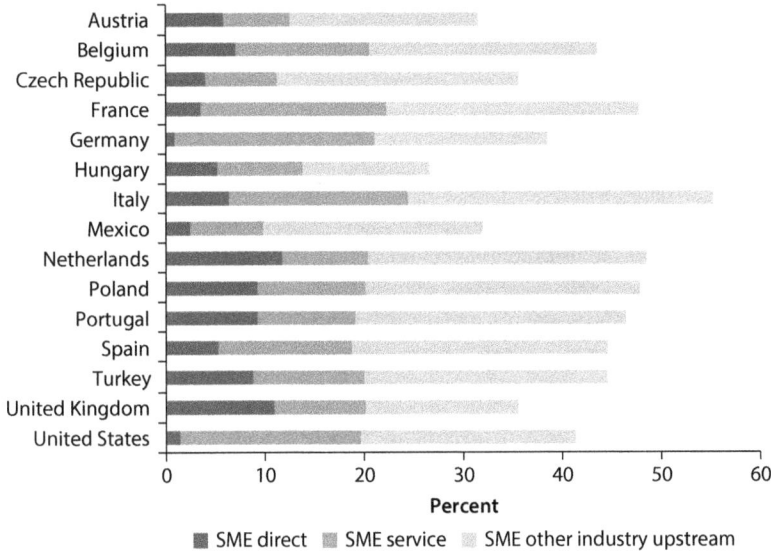

Sources: OECD/Eurostat Trade by Enterprise Characteristics database; OECD Structural and Demographic Business Statistics database; OECD Intercountry Input-Output Trade in the Value Added database.
Note: OECD = Organisation for Economic Co-operation and Development; SME = small and medium enterprise.

Figure 2.11 SME Share of Total Domestic Value Added of Exports of Business Services, 2009

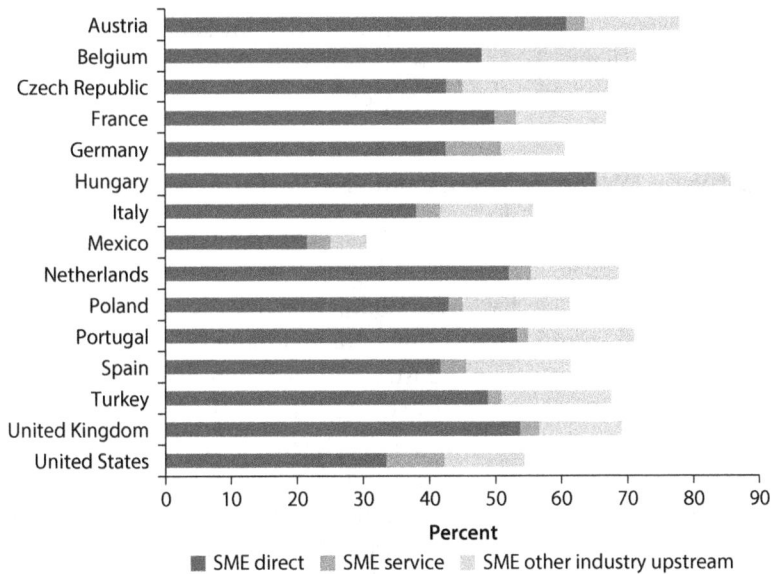

Sources: OECD/Eurostat Trade by Enterprise Characteristics database; OECD Structural and Demographic Business Statistics database; OECD Intercountry Input-Output Trade in the Value Added database.
Note: OECD = Organisation for Economic Co-operation and Development; SME = small and medium enterprise.

Figure 2.12 SME Share of Total Domestic Value Added of Exports of Manufacturing, 2009

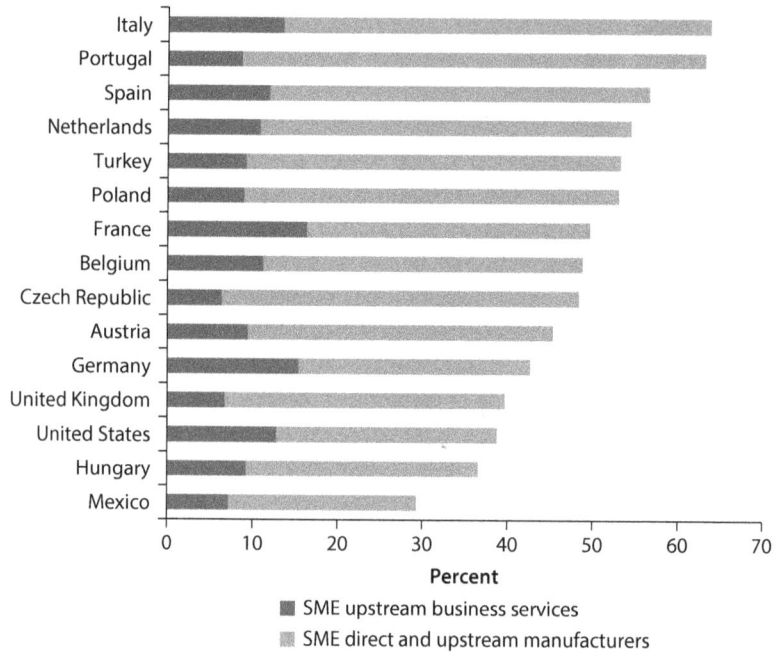

Sources: OECD/Eurostat Trade by Enterprise Characteristics database; OECD Structural and Demographic Business Statistics database; OECD Intercountry Input-Output Trade in the Value Added database.
Note: OECD = Organisation for Economic Co-operation and Development; SME = small and medium enterprise.

Finally, SME services contribute significantly to domestic value-added exports in manufacturing (figure 2.12), and more generally their contribution to downstream industries is significant across all countries.

Links between MNE Investments and SME Performance

Strong links between MNEs and their local suppliers tend to result in greater diffusion of knowledge, technology adoption, and know-how from foreign investors. GVCs, through backward links, generate demand and assistance effects in the host countries that in turn translate into diffusion of knowledge and technology in the supplier industry and increases in the availability and quality of inputs in the buyer industry. Lead firms tend to require more and better inputs from local suppliers and assist them through knowledge and technology sharing, advance payments, and other types of assistance. In this way, local suppliers receive incentives to upgrade their technology, and they may also diffuse knowledge to local firms. In addition, MNEs may provide higher-quality inputs to domestic clients. Competition between local firms may increase, and local firms may try to imitate the MNEs' products and practices. In addition, knowledge embodied in labor can transmit from foreign to local firms through labor turnover and MNE employees becoming entrepreneurs and creating their own start-ups.

Local sourcing is the critical channel for delivering positive spillovers. Supply chains, particularly backward links through local sourcing, appear to offer the most direct channel for short- and long-term gains from foreign direct investment (FDI) spillovers. Supply chains also tend to be the most visible and easiest to quantify, which increases their importance for policy makers. For example, in a World Bank survey of the mining sector, Farole and Winkler (2014) find that 33 percent of all surveyed local suppliers of foreign investors in Ghana and 42 percent in Chile started to export directly as a result of supplying foreign investors.

And behavior within the supply chain matters: the assistance of foreign investors to local supply chain partners has an important impact on spillover outcomes, so policies oriented to attract foreign investment are relevant to integrate SMEs in GVCs. Some of these policies include opening services sectors to private investment, removing investment incentives against local sources, and financing capacity building to help SMEs achieve the quality standards required by foreign firms. Although in some cases lead firms resist integration with a local supplier base, in other cases lead firms have an economic interest in developing a local support industry in producing countries, and actively pursue this objective. These findings suggest that it is possible to build meaningful links over time.

A clear finding from the surveys in the World Bank's Enterprise Surveys database is that foreign investors would much prefer not to have to rely on importing goods and services where there is cost-effective scope for domestic suppliers to compete and upgrade skills and standards, to benefit from face-to-face interactions and more responsive supply chains. Samsung, a company that has recently invested substantially in Vietnam, is actively attempting to grow a local supply base. In 2013, the company was one of the largest foreign investors in the country, with US$9 billion invested to date, and an additional US$3 billion smartphone factory under development. With a shortage of local suppliers,[1] Samsung has attempted to grow its Vietnamese supply base by organizing workshops in which it trains workers on the components it would like to make locally and audits the quality of specific suppliers. Samsung's next planned step is to organize a workshop in which it will invite its tier suppliers from other countries to meet with local firms to see if they can integrate them at a lower level in the supply chain (World Bank field interviews).

Despite the fact that in some industries, in particular some complex and sophisticated ones, MNEs have economic interests in creating links, productivity spillovers from FDI to the domestic economy in low-income countries remains limited. Farole and Winkler (2014) used a cross-section of more than 25,000 manufacturing firms in 78 low- and middle-income countries from the World Bank's Enterprise Surveys indicator database and found evidence of overall negative FDI spillovers. However, Farole and Winkler found that when an important share of FDI output is sold domestically and a larger share of local inputs is used, higher productivity spillovers arise for low- and medium-productivity domestic firms.

This evidence suggests that the impact of the local presence of MNEs on SMEs and firms in low-income countries is difficult to predict a priori. If the insertion of SMEs is concentrated in low-technology or labor-intensive tasks, the potential for spillovers may be limited. Moreover, foreign investors are less likely to provide assistance to local suppliers when supply contracts are ad hoc (rather than formalized and long term). It is also the case that global trends toward global supply chain management in companies are reducing opportunities for local supply participation at the high value-added end. With the most strategic and high-value purchases being coordinated at the global or regional level, for most low-income countries these impose significant limits on spillovers through domestic supply links.

Nevertheless, there are also opportunities that SMEs may be the first to reap. Short-term opportunities often come from outsourcing non-core activities, many of which are likely to be performed by SMEs. For example, according to the survey by Farole and Winkler (2014), in Lesotho and Swaziland, the most common activity provided by domestic suppliers was security services—beyond those were cleaning, basic maintenance, and catering. Longer-term opportunities may instead exist for SMEs that focus on the upstream end of the value chain. For example, in Sub-Saharan Africa, the provision of assistance to local suppliers was much more likely when the goods and services they provided were core parts of the upstream value chain. In the agribusiness sectors, the local firms that are most likely to receive assistance are those providing raw materials for agri-processing, and in the apparel sector, they are the cut-make-trim subcontractors. Limited series specialized orders are also more likely to be efficiently delivered by smaller firms.

The efforts of MNEs to provide assistance to local suppliers are often concentrated on their specific needs. For example, financial support would focus on meeting short-term working capital to avoid delays in production and delivery, but not on longer-term, patient, engaged types of finance, which would enable suppliers to invest in improving productivity and embedding spillover benefits.

The emphasis of MNEs on quality and standards represents an important area of potential for upgrading domestic firms, but support tends to be linked to compliance issues, such as health, safety, environment, and quality. However, even when quality and standards are firm specific, they are often built on global foundations and have the potential to upgrade the capacities of local suppliers, enabling them to serve other investors or start exporting. Although setting standards is important, direct technical assistance appears to be critical for supporting spillovers. Survey evidence indicates that demand effects alone—for example, requiring local suppliers to make specific changes to products or processes—may have a limited impact on spillovers in low-income countries. Instead, technical assistance, with or without the corresponding requirements of suppliers, resulted in greater spillovers. That finding suggests that although the proliferation of global standards within GVCs may create an opportunity for firm upgrading, most firms in low-income countries will require active support to take advantage of the opportunity.

Box 2.1 summarizes the take-away messages from this chapter. The next chapter provides an in-depth investigation of the challenges and constraints of participation in GVCs for SMEs.

Box 2.1 Key Take-Away Messages from Chapter 2

- The participation of small and medium enterprises (SMEs) in global value chains (GVCs) can be achieved by direct participation in exports (of goods and services that feed into third countries' production) or indirect participation by supplying other exporters.
- Direct participation of SMEs in the export of goods is limited, based on evidence from Organisation for Economic Co-operation and Development (OECD) countries and low-income countries.
- The majority of firms in most low-income countries is in the informal economy. Informality is one of the top five constraints for small firms in developing countries in doing business.
- Exporting SMEs are significantly underrepresented in (tangible) capital-intensive sectors, but compare favorably not only in the services sector, but also in heterogeneous manufacturing sectors where specialization and branding may be important.
- Exclusive focus on direct exports underestimates the participation of smaller firms in GVCs. Accounting for the direct and indirect contributions of SMEs to exports greatly reinforces their significance. In many OECD countries, for which such data are available, smaller firms account for more than half of the total exports of domestic value added, with much of it channeled through larger firms.
- Data on SMEs' labor productivity show that SMEs may integrate within GVCs at the two extremes of the value chain: in low value-added activities and high value-added activities. Survey evidence for low-income countries suggests that this is the case also in these countries—with a prevalence at the low value-added end of GVCs.
- The degree of upstream integration of SMEs varies widely across countries. Links between multinational enterprises (MNEs) and their local suppliers remain limited and difficult to achieve in low-income countries, even in those cases in which the MNEs have a business interest in developing a local supplier base and actively pursue that objective.
- Strong links between MNEs and their local suppliers tend to result in greater diffusion of knowledge, technology, and know-how from foreign investors. Yet, survey evidence suggests that the impact of the presence of MNEs on domestic firms in low-income countries, including SMEs, is difficult to predict a priori.
  - Short-term opportunities from MNE presence in low-income countries often come from outsourcing non-core activities, many of which are at the low end of the value chain and likely to be performed by SMEs.
  - Longer-term opportunities may instead exist for SMEs that focus on the upstream end of the value chain.
  - The emphasis of MNEs on certification of quality and standards represents an important area of potential for upgrading for domestic firms. But direct technical assistance appears to be critical for supporting spillovers through product and process upgrading and building skills that meet the standards and specifications of larger firms.

Note

1. Of the 61 suppliers servicing its factories in the country, only four are Vietnamese (*Việt Nam News* 2014).

References

Andrade, Gustavo Henrique, Miriam Bruhn, and David McKenzie. 2015. "A Helping Hand or the Long Arm of Law? Experimental Evidence on What Governments Can Do to Formalize Firms." *World Bank Economic Review* 30 (1): 24–54.

Bernard, Andrew B., J. Bradford Jensen, and Peter K. Schott. 2003. "Falling Trade Costs, Heterogeneous Firms, and Industry Dynamics." NBER Working Paper 9639, National Bureau of Economic Research, Cambridge, MA.

Bruhn, Miriam, and David McKenzie. 2014. "Entry Regulations and the Formalization of Microenterprises in Developing Countries." *World Bank Research Observer* 29 (2): 186–201.

Cebeci, Tolga, Ana M. Fernandes, Caroline Freund, and Martha Denisse Pierola. 2012. "Exporter Dynamics Database." Policy Research Working Paper 6229, World Bank, Washington, DC.

de Mel, Suresh, David McKenzie, and Christopher Woodruff. 2013. "The Demand for, and Consequences of, Formalization among Informal Firms in Sri Lanka." *American Economic Journal: Applied Economics* 5 (2): 122–50.

Farnworth, Cathy, and Jessica Hutchings. 2009. *Organic Agriculture and Women's Empowerment*. Bonn, Germany: IFOAM, Organics International.

Farole, Thomas, and Deborah Winkler. 2014. *Making Foreign Direct Investment Work for Sub-Saharan Africa*. Washington, DC: World Bank.

Mayer, Thierry, and Gianmarco Ottaviano. 2007. *The Happy Few: The Internationalization of European Firms*. Brussels: Bruegel Blueprint Series.

OECD (Organisation for Economic Co-operation and Development). 2015. *Entrepreneurship at a Glance*. Paris: OECD Publishing.

Slaughter, Matthew J. 2013. "American Companies and Global Supply Networks: Driving U.S. Economic Growth and Jobs by Connecting the World." U.S. Council for International Business and the United States Council Foundation, New York.

Staritz, Cornelia, and José Guilherme Reis. 2013. *Global Value Chains, Economic Upgrading, and Gender: Case Studies of the Horticulture, Tourism, and Call Center*. Washington, DC: World Bank.

USDA (United States Department of Agriculture). 2011a. "Organic Certification." Washington, DC: USDA. http://www.usda.gov/wps/portal/usda/usdahome?navid =ORGANIC_CERTIFICATIO.

———. 2011b. "Organica Agriculture: Organic Market Overview." Washington, DC: USDA. http://www.ers.usda.gov/briefing/organic/demand.htm.

USITC (United States International Trade Commission). 2010. *Small and Medium-Sized Enterprises: Characteristics and Performance*. USITC Publication 4189, Washington, DC.

Việt Nam News. 2014. "Samsung Chooses Few Vietnamese Suppliers." October 17. http:// vietnamnews.vn/economy/261534/samsung-chooses-few-vietnamese-suppliers.html.

CHAPTER 3

Participation of SMEs and Low-Income Countries in GVCs: Determinants and Challenges

Introduction

Informality is one of the top five constraints for small firms in low-income countries in doing business. Informality is also a binding constraint to integrating into global value chains (GVCs). In order to move into the formal economy, the broad key challenge for suppliers that want to integrate into GVCs, or that want to strengthen and upgrade their participation in GVCs, is to increase productivity and access the necessary knowledge and technology to compete. These firms, which include not only small and medium enterprises (SMEs) and larger firms in low-income countries, but also many SMEs in high-income countries, are often suppliers of low or high value-added intermediate products, which they sell on international markets. Productivity is key to selling at internationally competitive prices (OECD 2008, 2015a).[1] Broadening the skill set and innovating and accessing foreign technology allow SMEs and firms in low-income countries to increase productivity and upgrade.

This upgrading takes several forms, as illustrated in figure 3.1. Starting from the tasks in which firms in a country have a comparative advantage, based on current skills, capabilities, and capital endowments, the country can achieve higher value added (and hence productivity growth and economic growth) through a variety of channels (OECD 2013a). For example, firms can increase productivity in the current tasks of comparative advantage. They can do so by *process upgrading*; this is the manner through which firms acquire capabilities to process tasks with significantly higher efficiency and lower defect rates. *Product upgrading* takes place when firms acquire capabilities to supply higher value-added goods compared with those provided by rivals. Product upgrading can occur through the adoption of cutting-edge technologies, investments in research and development (R&D), and vertical and horizontal innovation. *Functional upgrading* occurs instead when firms acquire capabilities in more technologically

Figure 3.1 What Types of Economic Upgrading?

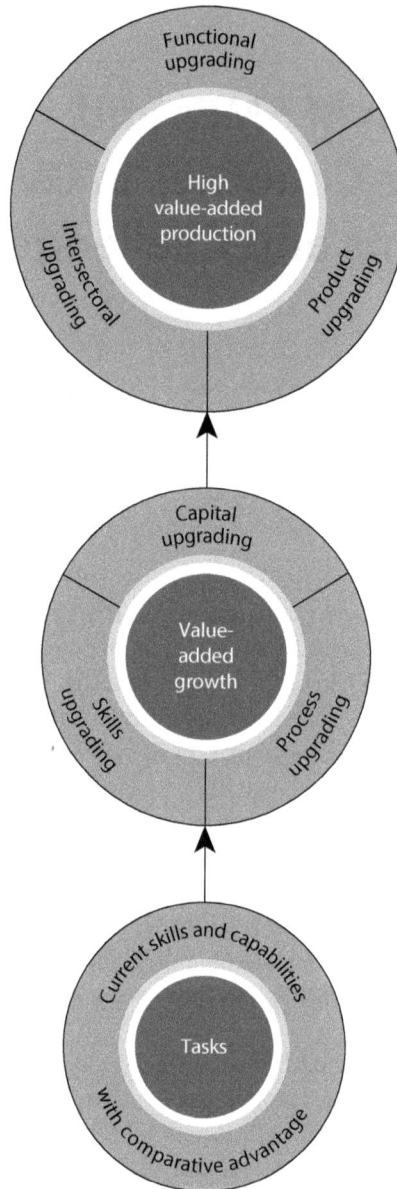

Functional
upgrading

Intersectoral
upgrading

High
value-added
production

Product
upgrading

Capital
upgrading

Skills
upgrading

Value-
added
growth

Process
upgrading

Current skills and capabilities

Tasks

with comparative advantage

Source: Taglioni and Winkler 2016.

sophisticated, human capital rich, or integrated functions and segments of a GVC, which are associated with higher value-added production. Functional upgrading is to be distinguished from *inter-sector upgrading*, which occurs when firms acquire capabilities, often leveraging the knowledge and skills acquired in the current chain, to participate in *new* GVCs, producing higher value-added products or services (see figure 3.2 for an example of inter-sector upgrading).

Figure 3.2 Example for Possible Inter-Sector Upgrading in Nicaragua

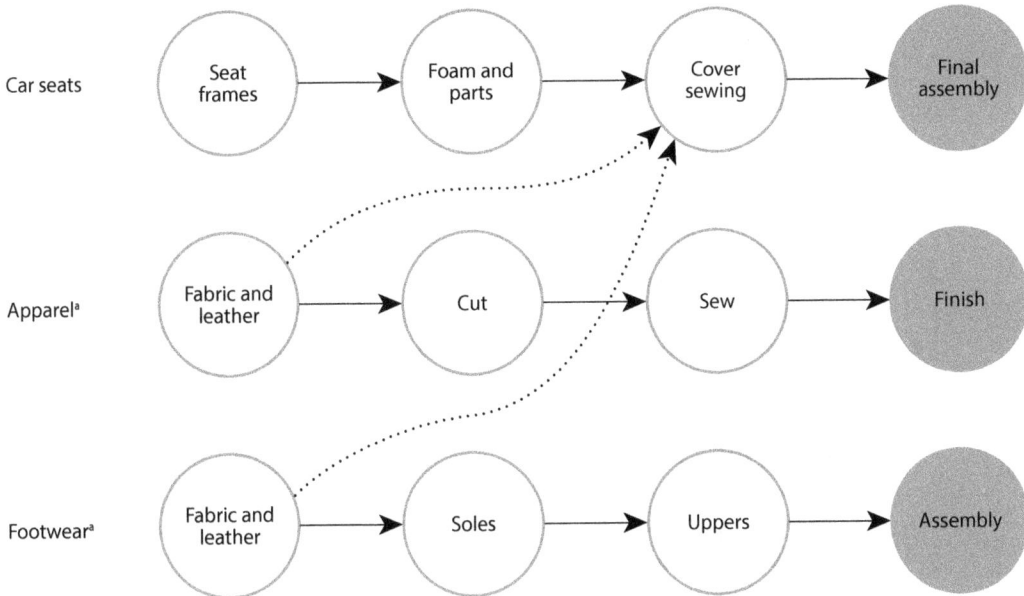

Source: Taglioni and Winkler 2016.
a. Industry value chains that are currently active in Nicaragua.

Firms—not countries or governments—are the main actors in value chains. Firms participate in GVCs first and foremost to make a profit, and do so when it is in their business interest. The theory of comparative advantage teaches that firms can obtain gains from GVCs through specialization. However, these gains do not necessarily require producing more sophisticated or technology-intensive products. Value chains offer the opportunity to insert into the increasingly fragmented segments of the production of an array of products, tasks, or functions that are needed; this is where SMEs can engage in fruitful participation. Determining which segments of the value chain will be profitable is a matter of the characteristics of the production process and the relative skills and resource endowments of the firms (that is, the comparative advantage) (OECD 2008).

Recently, and perhaps mistakenly, the concept of upgrading has been seen as the need to capture a growing domestic share of a product's value.[2] This narrow view of upgrading may miss the point: the *volume* of the activity matters just as much, or more, as the share of the product. For example, although it is true that the manufacture of garments is a relatively labor-intensive process that amounts to a small share of the total value of the final product (relative to the design and commercialization segments), it is also true that important benefits can be derived by SMEs from specializing in such manufacturing activities and aiming at performing them on a larger scale.

The case of specialization in electronics in Asia is illustrative of this. Several firms have become assemblers of electronic devices par excellence and have attracted clients that include, among others, Apple, Dell, Amazon, Nokia, and Samsung.

When considering the total value of products made by those lead firms, an average share of 5 percent of the value adds up to a relatively large sum. Although the assemblers could have instead launched a new mobile phone to rival the larger smartphone producers (as an alternative business development strategy), thereby seeking to enter the higher end of the smiley curve to capture larger shares of the value of the final product, they would have had to capture a significant market share from the established electronic device producers to succeed. From this perspective, it is therefore important to recognize the economic value that is created by the activities of the assembling or manufacturing firm, and not simply focus on the share that the firm occupies in the value of the final product. Similarly, SMEs in low-income countries should aim to move up the value chain by seeking to enhance their productivity and grow their volume of activities.

A good illustration of some of the pitfalls associated with defining upgrading relative to the share rather than the value added to a product is the case of Vietnam's production of electrical and optical equipment. As can be seen in figure 3.3, the domestic content of Vietnam's electrical and optical equipment exports fell from 44.7 to 30.8 percent between 1995 and 2011, but the volume of domestic value added embodied in exports increased more than 20-fold. Although other developments in the Vietnamese and global economies that are not accounted for may have played a role, these figures provide evidence that firms operating in Vietnam have increased the foreign content of their products while multiplying their overall sales, profits, and the wage bill for the workers they employ.

Figure 3.3 Enjoying a Smaller Share of a Larger Pie: Electrical and Optical Equipment in Vietnam

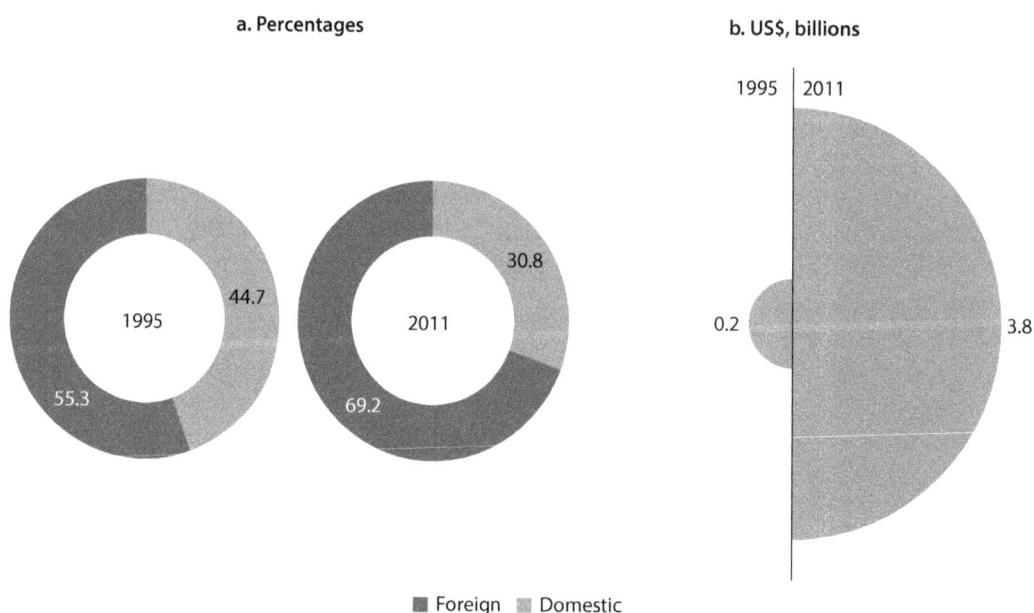

a. Percentages

b. US$, billions

■ Foreign ▨ Domestic

Source: Organisation for Economic Co-operation and Development–World Trade Organization Trade in Value Added database, 2015 update.

Lessons can also be learned from looking at the determinants of movements along the value chain (OECD 2015a; Taglioni and Winkler 2016). Positive changes in foreign sourcing are associated with positive changes in the per capita domestic value added in exports, which suggests that a greater use of foreign inputs is complementary to growing per capita domestic value added in exports. Similarly, countries' value chain activity (the share of foreign value added in exports) is linked to growing sophistication and diversification of exports, as is the use of more sophisticated inputs. This, a priori, suggests that SMEs should benefit from policies that reduce the costs of accessing foreign intermediate goods so that tariff reductions and other accompanying policy measures aimed at reducing trading costs (such as trade facilitation and development of national infrastructure) are likely to matter for SMEs in low-income countries.

A particularly important driver for upgrading in GVCs is investment in knowledge-based capital (KBC). The highest level of value creation in a GVC is often found in certain upstream activities, such as new concept development, design, R&D, or the manufacturing of key parts and components, as well as in certain downstream activities, such as marketing, branding, or customer service. Such activities involve tacit, non-codified knowledge in areas such as original design, the creation and management of cutting-edge technology, and complex systems, as well as management or organizational know-how.

Investments in KBC not only drive productivity growth, they also determine the extent to which the final product of a value chain can be differentiated in consumer markets, which in turn determines the total value the GVC can create. For example, much of the success of recent Apple products is due to design features. The value that a firm creates within a GVC also depends on the difficulty for rivals to supply similar or substitutable products. When a product is easy to replicate, for example, when it is not tacit or not protected by intellectual property rights (IPRs), rival firms can easily develop substitutes for the inputs that a firm provides to a GVC.

Different types of KBC play a role in GVCs, and there are three main categories (OECD 2013b): (a) computerized information (software and databases); (b) innovative property (R&D and non-R&D innovative expenditures, including copyrights, designs, and trademarks); and (c) economic competencies (brand equity, firm-specific technological and managerial skills, networks, and organizational structures). A recent survey of Japanese firms, for example, emphasizes the importance of economic and managerial competencies for competitiveness, notably manufacturing skills, brand and customer recognition, and agile and flexible organization (figure 3.4). The Japanese firms that are the most engaged in GVCs—those with exports or imports of intermediate goods and those that own offshore plants—consider such competencies to be more important than firms without trade or foreign plants. These firms also put greater emphasis on cutting-edge technology and "big data" as sources of competitive advantage than firms oriented toward the domestic market.

Further, compliance with international standards is a relevant challenge for SMEs to enter into GVCs. Consumers and final-good producers around the

Figure 3.4 The Relevance of Various Forms of KBC to the Competitiveness of Japanese Manufacturing Firms
(% of firms indicating each KBC as the essential factor contributing to their competitiveness or profitability)

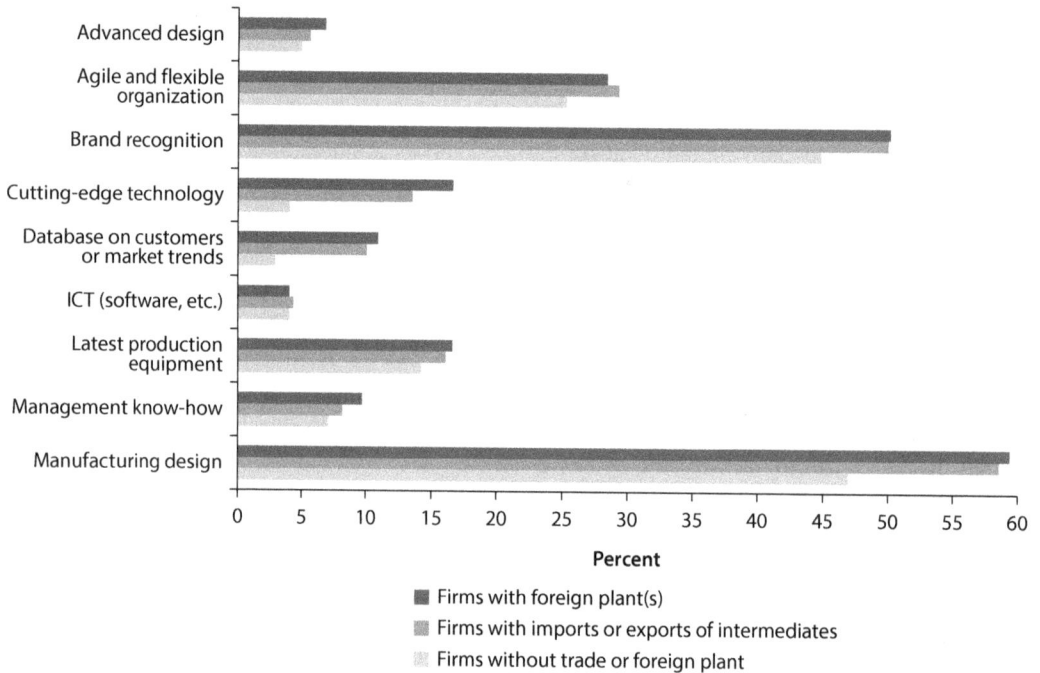

Source: Ministry of Economy, Trade, and Industry (Japan) 2012.
Note: The shares do not add up to 100 percent because firms are allowed to select multiple forms of KBC that they consider essential. The figure shows the share of firms that indicate the form of KBC concerned to be essential to competitiveness. ICT = information and communication technology; KBC = knowledge-based capital.

world increasingly demand products and services that are simultaneously good for the economy, the environment, and society—the triple bottom line approach to sustainable growth. Indeed, low labor and production costs are often insufficient motivation for lead firms to invest and source from SMEs in low-income countries. The ability to adhere to environmental, labor, and quality standards matters greatly, especially for SMEs, which typically face more difficulty in meeting the standards than large companies, and for firms in low-income countries, which typically face more difficulties in meeting them than firms in high-income countries (box 3.1).

But apart from standards, in general terms, there are internal and external factors that help SMEs overcome the challenges and participate in GVCs. Internal factors affect SMEs' capabilities to supply low and high value-added intermediate products at low cost, including innovation, technology adoption, managerial capacity, and workforce skills. External factors involve trade issues, the business environment, and the investment climate. Although both sets of drivers are very important, the focus of this report is on identifying areas for collective policy action. Therefore, the next section provides a brief account of the internal determinants, while the main focus of the discussion is on external determinants.

Box 3.1 The World Bank's Work to Strengthen Developing Countries' Ability to Meet International Product and Process Standards

The World Bank Group is working to strengthen its global partnerships with governments, businesses, consumer and labor groups, and other international organizations to help small and medium enterprises to comply with product and process standards. An inclusive partnership approach opens the door to the best insights and most successful models from those with experience in raising standards, improving productivity, developing skills, and spreading prosperity through participation in global value chains.

The Better Work Program—a partnership between the World Bank Group's International Finance Corporation and the International Labour Organization—exemplifies how partnerships can make an impact. Better Work began in 2007 in response to demand from consumers and multinational firms for better standards in garment factories. The program has helped to improve the lives of more than 1 million garment workers in eight countries, by helping management and labor work together to provide safe, clean, and equitable working environments.

Internal Determinants of SME Participation and Upgrading in GVCs

Innovation and Technology Adoption

For SMEs, innovation is an important requirement for successful participation in GVCs (OECD 2008). Process and organizational innovation increases firm productivity by reducing production costs and allowing firms to achieve the minimum level of efficiency required to cover fixed exporting costs. Product innovation creates learning-by-doing effects and helps SMEs offer new and upgraded products, while marketing innovation and innovative branding strategies allow SMEs to differentiate their products from those of their competitors and gain market share in GVCs. Innovative SMEs are more likely to participate in international markets than other firms are (figure 3.5).

A particularly important dimension related to innovation is the ability of SMEs to protect their intellectual assets (OECD 2011b). IPRs are instrumental for SMEs for several reasons: (a) to protect their innovations; (b) to position themselves competitively vis-à-vis larger enterprises in global markets; (c) to signal current and prospective value competitors and partners, which can help enhance access to finance; (d) to access knowledge markets and networks; (e) to open up new commercial pathways; and (f) to segment existing markets.

Given that SMEs lack internal financial resources, IPRs are particularly attractive because of the role they can play in facilitating access to finance. That role can arise through three channels: (a) as a signaling device for financial markets, (b) as collateral to obtain financing, and (c) as a direct source of finance through licensing. A survey of firms undertaken by the European Patent Office indicates that SMEs are much more likely to patent for financial reasons, rather than as a means to protect against imitation (de Rassenfosse and Wastin 2011). Of the SMEs

Figure 3.5 SMEs Participating in International Markets, by Innovation Status, 2010 to 2012
(% of firms in the relevant group)

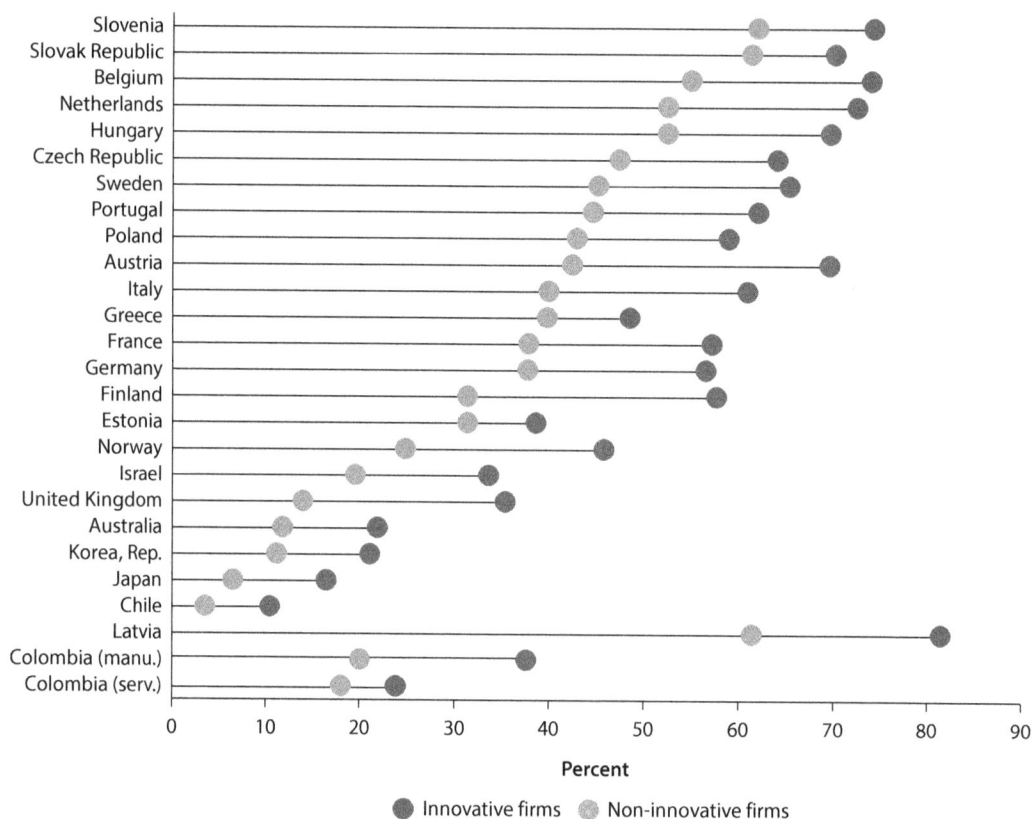

Source: OECD 2015c.

Note: International comparability may be limited because of differences in innovation survey methodologies and country-specific response patterns. European countries follow harmonized survey guidelines with the CIS. CIS = Community Innovation Survey; SMEs = small and medium enterprises.

surveyed, 40 percent had strong "monetary motivations" to apply, that is, attracting investors or licensing. By contrast, that proportion is as low as 15 percent for large applicant firms. This finding indicates that lowering transaction costs for IPRs and increasing their signaling value (that is, by encouraging high-quality examinations) would likely be particularly valuable for SMEs. OECD (2015a) provides a discussion on this topic.

Governments that are keen on generating development from GVC participation tend to pass rigorous IPR legislation, while at the same time providing assistance to SMEs, for example, through e-learning tools that help domestic firms commercialize their intellectual property. Governments also assist SMEs in the use of freely available technologies or the acquisition of technological licensing agreements. Morocco provides such assistance through the Office Marocain de la Propriété Industrielle in the framework of its Horizon 2015 program (Taglioni and Winkler 2016).

Further, firms have much to gain by adopting new technologies. Technology adoption and knowledge absorption are particularly important priorities for SMEs in low-income countries. The acquisition and use of existing knowledge is less costly and less risky than is the creation of new processes or products, while the productivity rewards can be substantial. Cooperation with foreign partners, upstream and downstream, is critical in this respect and can improve firm efficiency, because SMEs can obtain substantial benefits in information flow, technology transfer, learning opportunities, and imitation or demonstration effects that occur in the context of interactions with suppliers and clients. Cooperation with universities or other knowledge institutions can be helpful too; these are sometimes associated with greater diffusion of foreign technologies (OECD 2015a).

For example, the technologies that foreign companies frequently use are not always available in domestic markets. Domestic firms sometimes imitate foreign technologies to increase production efficiency and supply intermediate goods at a lower price (Blomström and Kokko 1998). Alternatively, domestic firms use the new technology to produce high-quality products at low cost. Formal or informal contact with affiliates of foreign firms also provides information about the pros and cons of using particular technologies, and creates productivity spillovers (Javorcik 2004; Rodríguez-Clare 1996; Wang and Blomström 1992). In addition, demonstration externalities help SMEs acquire the knowledge needed to use more efficient production techniques. These effects are most prominent in tightly organized supply chains, where the local supply base is large and fragmented.

Foreign investors have an incentive to promote demonstration effects when providing individual technical assistance is prohibitive or inefficient. This approach is most apparent in the agribusiness value chain, where foreign investors actively promote demonstration effects by supporting the upgrading of their suppliers through the establishment of demonstration plots and nucleus farms. However, spillovers from demonstration plots are constrained by limited collaboration between foreign investors and domestic firms in the same sector. The findings from survey work in Sub-Saharan Africa (Farole and Winker 2014) indicate that in most countries in the region, sector collaboration is weak, particularly between foreign-owned and domestic firms. Of the three sectors studied by Farole and Winkler, only agribusiness showed any significant levels of collaboration between foreign firms and the domestic sector, particularly through links with national training centers and research institutes.

Fostering innovation and technology adoption is not always easy, and—to a large extent—success depends on the structural features of individual GVCs. In an attempt to facilitate innovation and technology adoption from foreign direct investment (FDI) in the automotive sector to local firms, Invest in Macedonia, the investment agency of the Former Yugoslav Republic of Macedonia, has tried to encourage global suppliers in the automotive sector to bring their own suppliers into the country. The idea is that global suppliers (Tier 1) might guarantee their smaller suppliers (Tier 2 and Tier 3) a significant amount of work though long-term contracts in return for colocating. In exchange, these firms might be more open to forming strategic partnerships with the local automotive cluster, which is also composed predominantly of SMEs. However, small suppliers generally do not have the resources or market incentives to internationalize production. Moreover, suppliers of basic inputs (such as chemicals, semiconductors, wire, metals, and plastics) tend to be large and serve a broad customer base, but they have capital-intensive production facilities with very high minimum scale requirements. As a result, they tend to supply customers regionally and globally from a handful of production locations.

Managerial Skills and Workforce Capacity

SMEs in low-income countries are generally plagued by weak managerial skills and inefficient organization. Those weaknesses are reflected in low levels of productivity, suboptimal use of their workforce, waste of materials and inputs, and poor efficiency at the level of the production floor (Iacovone and Qasim 2013). Management can be thought of as a technology (Bloom, Sadun, and Van Reenen 2013), with empirical evidence suggesting that raising managerial quality could significantly raise productivity (Andrews and Criscuolo 2013; figure 3.6). A competitive and open business environment tends to favor the adoption of superior

Figure 3.6 Managerial Quality Differs across Countries, with Important Implications for Productivity

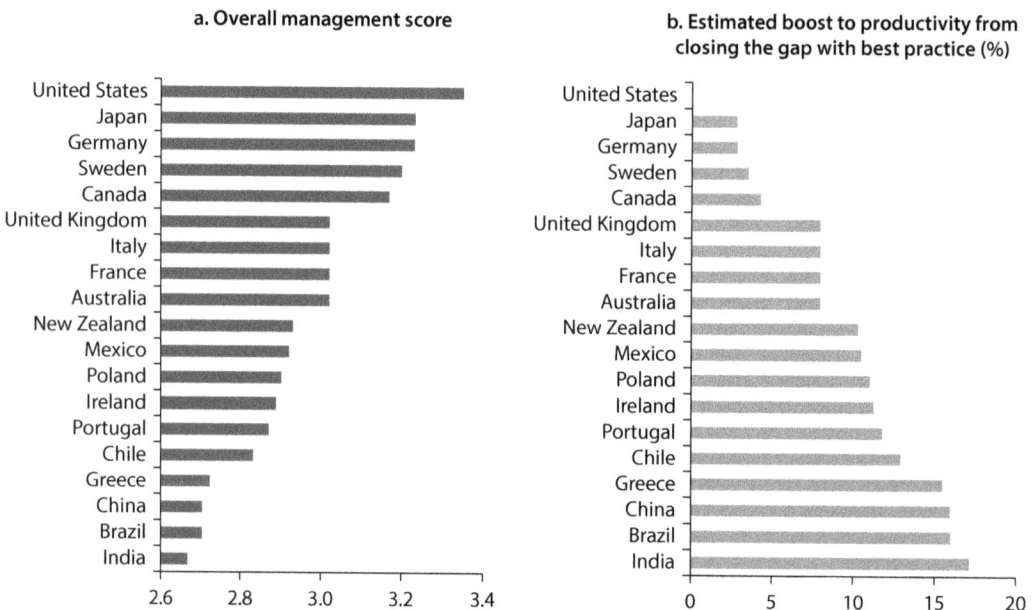

Sources: Andrews and Criscuolo 2013; based on the management scores and estimated coefficients in Bloom et al. 2012.
Note: The overall management score is an average of responses to 18 survey questions that are designed to reveal the extent to which firms: (a) monitor what goes on inside the firm and use this information for continuous improvement; (b) set targets and track outcomes; and (c) effectively utilize incentive structures (for example, promote and rewarding employees based on performance). The estimates in panel b are calculated from the difference in management scores between each country and the United States and the estimated coefficient on the management score term in a firm-level regression of sales on management scores, capital, and employment. The sample is based on medium-size firms, ranging from 50 to 10,000 employees.

managerial practices and reduces incentives for maintaining inefficient business structures (for example, via inheritance tax exemptions that may prolong the existence of poorly managed family-owned firms), thus facilitating within-firm productivity improvements (OECD 2015d).

Specifically, the ability and capacity of the entrepreneur to implement a business plan largely determine the success or failure of a firm at creation and during growth. Further, a skilled workforce is a relevant determinant of firm productivity. Nevertheless, acquiring the right mix of skills, ideas, and talents is a challenge for entrepreneurs, especially in markets where the required skills are scarce or expensive. Even where the skills are available, ensuring that the right mix of skills is matched to an entrepreneurial venture requires reducing information asymmetry about skill sets and effective contracting mechanisms that guarantee the efficient allocation of skills and talent across firms (Iacovone and Qasim 2013). Relatively high rates of skills mismatch in many countries point to rigidities in labor market matching that reduce resource reallocation and constrain the growth of young and innovative SMEs (OECD 2015d).

Foreign investors make relatively greater use of local skilled staff than they do of local suppliers in low-income countries, but the practice varies significantly across countries. In Chile's mining sector, for example, 70–80 percent of workers in skilled positions are local, whereas across surveyed African countries, the share is 30–50 percent. In agribusiness, 75–85 percent of management, supervisory, and technical workers in Kenya and Vietnam are local, whereas the figures are 1–10 percentage points lower in Ghana and Mozambique. Finally, in apparel, although more than 33 percent of management and technical staff is local in Kenya, less than 20 percent is local in Swaziland.

The employment of local skilled labor is constrained by supply. Survey results from several low-income countries indicate that by far the largest constraint perceived by foreign investors to hiring more local staff in technical and managerial positions is the lack of skilled labor. Field interviews of GVC firms in Vietnam, for instance, suggest that the local education system is poorly suited to the modern international business environment. Education in foreign languages and *soft* business skills (presentations, team work, and business planning, as well as sales and marketing) were found to be critical deficiencies. Branding, marketing, and retail services are necessary for brand development in apparel production, for example. Low-income countries that target upward graduation in this sector will need to enhance the capacity of firms in branding, marketing, and retail services, for the domestic market and overseas markets as well. The problem is particularly severe for SMEs. Within these firms, branding and marketing are generally performed in-house with few resources invested in those activities. And for most, these tasks are done by "merchandising teams," which are responsible for organizing orders from clients, rather than "sales and marketing teams."

The lack of foreign language skills in many low-income countries is also a serious impediment to GVC-driven growth. For example, in the case of Vietnam, Japan is an increasingly important software outsourcing market. Vietnam recently overtook India as the second largest exporter of software services to Japan.

The lack of Japanese language skills in Vietnam could dampen demand and the sector's future growth. Vietnam has a similar, if less severe, problem with the U.S. market, which requires English language skills.

Localizing skilled positions may sometimes also be hindered by FDI corporate culture. Foreign investors continue to reserve certain functions for foreign workers and suppliers that colocate with them, for reasons of corporate culture; when there is a significant language gap between the host country and the foreign investors; or when the costs of supporting foreign workers and suppliers (including relocation costs) are relatively low. The Nigerian oil industry, for example, has failed over the years to provide significant employment for local populations. The lack of job opportunities combined with the demise of fishing—because of pollution from the oil industry—has translated into increased poverty and, eventually, social unrest.

The difficulties notwithstanding, broadening the skill set in a country is possible. Some countries have managed to leverage their initial low-cost advantage to retool their workforce toward higher skills, using public institutions. That is the case, for example, in Costa Rica and FYR Macedonia. The latter—with an unemployment rate of 30 percent and a large segment of the labor force suited for basic production work without extensive training—initially attracted FDI because of its cheap labor. According to World Bank field interviews, one company, assessing the opportunity to locate in the country, had concerns about the quality of the labor force. Before its full commitment, it met with the faculty of electrical and mechanical engineering at the University of Skopje, which it found was open to collaborating with the company. A program has been established since then to allow students the opportunity to spend their senior year on a curriculum that teaches skills relevant to the company's in-country activities. The company has worked closely with the university in other ways as well, financing one of its laboratories and creating a scholarship program to finance studies for some engineering students. A 10- to 12-week summer internship is another part of that collaborative effort. The program offers students summer employment and full-time permanent employment upon graduation if they have satisfied the program's requirements. Following the example of this first company, other FDI established similar programs. As a result, the availability of high technical skills is now considered one of the factors of the attractiveness of FYR Macedonia.

Shared Value in Low-Income Countries and SMEs

Not all GVCs are accessible to low-income countries and SMEs. Globalized industries, with cutting-edge technology, may not be the best entry point for the poorest among low-income countries to integrate into GVCs. Gold, tantalum (also commonly referred to as *coltan*), tin, and tungsten—four minerals with a large production base in Sub-Saharan Africa—are necessary for the functionality or production of various products, including integrated circuits, assembled products, and evaluation boards, which, depending on the product, contain one or more of these minerals (top left corner in figure 3.7). The imports of these

Figure 3.7 The ICT GVC

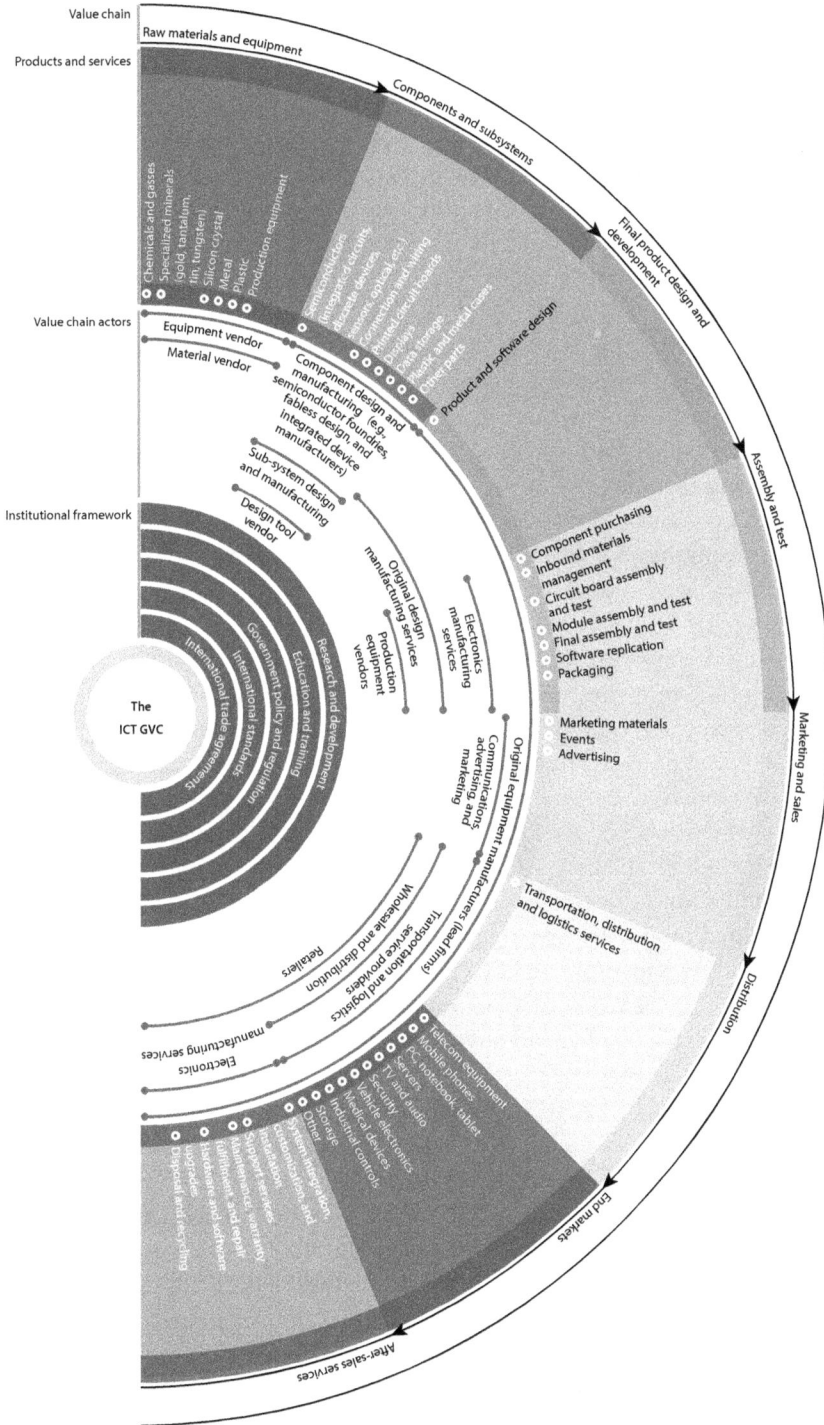

Source: Sturgeon et al. 2013.
Note: GVC = global value chain; ICT = information and communication technology.

minerals are very concentrated: China and Malaysia cover more than 80 percent of the total world imports of tin; China; Hong Kong SAR, China; Thailand; and the United States cover more than 90 percent of the global imports of tantalum. The process of bringing such metals to an exploitable form usually includes mining, separation, refining, fabrication of alloys, and final manufacturing in the components.

Building the capacity to create more local content from the industries exploiting these minerals may therefore be very difficult for countries that lack the skills to process such minerals and are subject to frequent power outages. In addition to being costly, the economic return of such endeavor is also very difficult to predict.

Meanwhile, focusing on creating domestic value in areas closer to the technology frontier of the producing country may have higher payoffs in spillovers to the domestic economy and to a broad base of domestic producers. This objective can be reached in several ways, including by improving the quality of products and production in sectors of comparative advantage, identifying market-based mechanisms and business models that foster more local value creation, strengthening the domestic absorptive capacity, and diversifying the local supply. SMEs and low-income countries should aim for the following:

- Pursuing disruptive and technological innovations that have market potential to produce higher value products and to overcome the challenges they necessitate. Case in point: Rwanda's efforts to upgrade its coffee production, which is one of its major agricultural exports. In 2003, an aggressive strategy was developed to increase total exports of coffee and move the industry into high-quality, specialty end markets. The major efforts that have been put in place include participation in international exhibitions, demonstrations, contests, and above all strict quality control. Two long-term, donor-funded projects helped producers develop buyer-seller relationships and helped growers raise quality. Aid projects have also helped farmers form cooperatives to meet the requirements of "fair trade" coffee and experiment with organic and shade-grown coffees, all of which command a substantial premium over ordinary coffee. Increased access to washing stations increased the farmers' income by up to 55 percent. Washing and grading the coffee cherries have made it possible to obtain prices for products of higher quality, giving farmers an incentive to increase quality. Regulatory reform has also allowed individual Rwandese cooperatives and private owners to negotiate directly with specialty roasters in Europe and the United States, enabling them to sell at more than twice the market rate (Nielsen 2008).

- Identifying market-based mechanisms and business models that by construction create more value in producing countries is also a paying strategy. An ongoing World Bank project in Haiti is supporting 10 local development teams with capacity-building and specific financing tools. The objective is to create "shared value alliances" of local farmers or small manufacturers and international logistics companies to increase their share of value in the mango, avocado, coffee, and garment GVCs.

- Strengthening the domestic absorptive capacity, including through a well-targeted supplier program, is also likely to help. The Czech Supplier Development Program was designed by the World Bank Foreign Investment Advisory Services in 1999. The first round of the Czech program was implemented by CzechInvest using pre-accession European Union Phare funding of US$4 million in 2000–02. The program aimed to connect Czech suppliers to GVCs and increase local content in the electronics sector in the first phase. Later phases focused on the automotive and aerospace sectors. The first phase of the program involved 32 multinational companies and 48 SMEs that received training and intensive consultancy services. An independent evaluation undertaken 18 months after the end of the pilot showed that 15 companies had gained new business that they attributed to the program, with those contracts worth US$18 million annually in 2003. Four companies had also found new companies abroad, and three companies had obtained contracts with higher value-added content. The World Bank teams have used their experience advising the Government of Costa Rica, developing a loan project in Kazakhstan, and providing technical assistance to FYR Macedonia.

External Determinants of SME Participation in GVCs

Although firm capabilities are crucial to determine the participation of SMEs in GVCs, external conditions are equally relevant, as they can facilitate or impede participation in GVCs. Understanding the determinants of GVC participation is a first step in unraveling how governments can target their policies to spread the gains of GVC participation to the wider population. These determinants can be subsumed into two broad categories: (a) factors that are not easily influenced by policy, at least in the short to medium term, and (b) factors that can be reflected in measures such as trade and investment openness. Importantly, since structural characteristics differ widely across countries, the level of participation across countries cannot simply be compared to say that a country with higher participation is "doing better" in GVCs. Larger countries, for example, tend to have lower rates of participation, which is attributed to the fact that they have larger domestic markets from which to draw their intermediate goods and services.

Market size, the level of development, industrial structure, and location are some of the main determinants of aggregate GVC participation, but trade and other policies can also play a significant role. Low import tariffs, at home and in export markets; engagement in regional trade agreements; inward FDI openness; trade facilitation; logistics performance; infrastructure; intellectual property protection; and the quality of regulations and institutions can all facilitate GVC engagement (Kowalski et al. 2015).

As far as firms' perceptions are concerned, a survey on Aid for Trade conducted jointly by the Organisation for Economic Co-operation and Development

Figure 3.8 Barriers Faced by Firms in Entering Value Chains: Private Sector Views

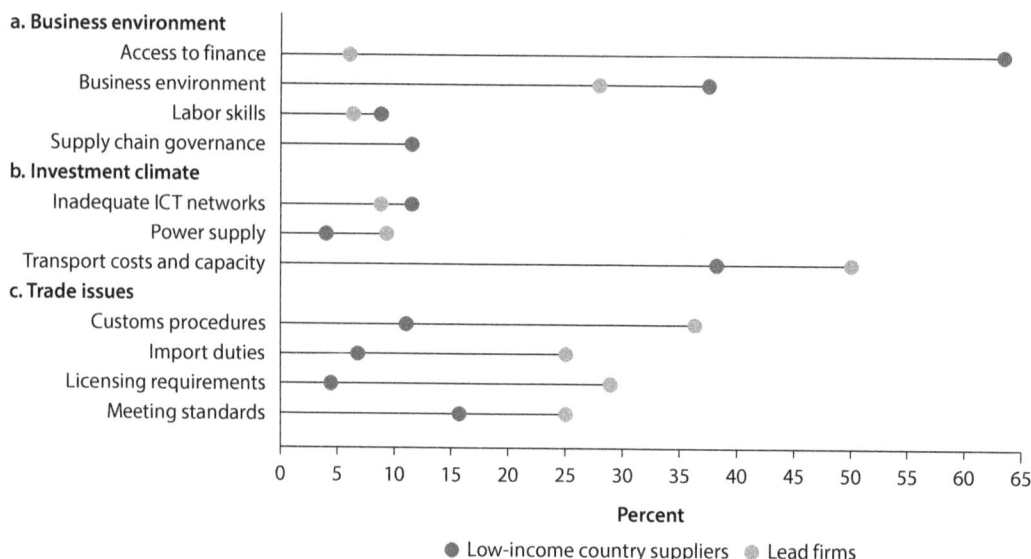

Source: OECD and WTO 2013.
Note: ICT = information and communication technology.

(OECD) and the World Trade Organization (WTO) in 2013, shows that for suppliers from low-income countries, access to finance (in particular, trade finance) is the main obstacle preventing them from entering, establishing, or moving up in value chains (figure 3.8). The suppliers also cited transportation and shipping costs, inadequate infrastructure, and regulatory uncertainty (often tied to a complex business environment) as major obstacles, together with a lack of labor force skills. Among lead firms, customs procedures ranked high as a particular obstacle to bringing suppliers in low-income countries into their value chains, as well as standards compliance issues. Informal practices and payment requests were also cited as of particular concern in their relationships with suppliers.

Access to External Sources of Funding[3]

Access to external sources of funding is critical to finance SMEs that want to participate in GVCs; however, this implies overcoming several obstacles. The first obstacles have nothing specifically to do with value chains, but they make banks and many financial institutions reluctant to lend to SMEs. The way banks, in particular, approach credit underwriting and portfolio management makes SMEs expensive and difficult to acquire as clients, and equally expensive and difficult to serve. SMEs' business is too small to support the heavy hand-holding approach banks use for corporate finance, and SMEs do not have the Bloomberg screen-ready, third-party rating and other information corporate bankers need to see, nor audited accounts (nor any decent accounts, in many cases).

In most emerging markets (and in many OECD markets), SMEs and their entrepreneurs have no credit report, because they have never borrowed from a formal financial institution. Further, size and the intangibility of assets, in particular for young, innovative SMEs, play against the creditworthiness ratings of many SMEs. Creditworthiness is indeed still mostly based on the evaluation of a company's assets and liabilities recorded on its balance sheet. Routinely, banks rely on past performance, current turnover, and liquidity of the firm as predictors for repayment ability. For the most part, company valuations based on a company's balance sheet do not include the potential for future earnings in their decision-making processes. They fail to take into account the intrinsic worth of the firm's know-how, pool of talent, distribution channels, business relationships, business model, access to technology, and so forth. Assessing creditworthiness based on past balance sheet data is increasingly an archaic measure of the true intrinsic value of a firm, particularly for service-oriented firms, start-ups, and GVC suppliers.

Limitations to securing movable assets in financial transactions pose a fundamental obstacle to value chain finance development in many countries, including many Group of Twenty (G20) nations. The Financial Stability Board designated the World Bank's Insolvency and Creditor Rights standard and the United Nations Commission on International Trade Law Legislative Guides as best practices for protecting creditor rights. However, many G20 nations fall short of best practice standards in this area. Some G20 countries still use document registration, requiring delivery and recording of pledge agreements (and sometimes other documents) at the registry, instead of the recommended "notice" system. Other countries do not use a centralized registry or single registry for all types of movable assets. Some European Union countries still require physical appearance by one or both parties before the registry to register security interests. Even within the European Union and other regional economic entities, there has been little harmonization of practice to date in this area. Given the limitations of the G20 and high-income country regimes, it is small wonder that few emerging market countries present encouraging environments for using movables as collateral.[4]

Banks and other financial institutions' comfort with supply chain financing will increase as they gain greater information on transactions in those chains, reducing information asymmetries in the SME market. This necessitates access to such nonconventional financial/credit information, which is not always supported in countries' credit information regimes, particularly in countries that have a dominant central registry operated by a government agency. This agency, often the central bank, can face political obstacles as it seeks to add new supply chain data, which may fall under the purview of a different ministry (Industry and Trade, Economy, or Commerce, for example). Even in countries where private credit information aggregators are present, new, post-Snowden regulations have been tightening conditions for data access. Although consumer privacy rights must be protected, care should be taken to ensure an appropriate balance between this protection and the economic/employment benefits of greater SME access to financing.

The implementation of Basel II/III, which already caused a ripple in trade finance systems before the European Union Capital Requirements Directive IV allowed for more appropriate credit conversion factors, will pose additional challenges for banks looking to increase supply chain financing. The World Bank Group's February-March 2015 survey of 53 emerging market regulators for the Basel Consultative Group found that most believe the Basel II revisions on credit risk will have an adverse influence on lending to SMEs. The regulators felt that the treatment of SME exposures not qualifying for inclusion in retail portfolios was one of the main areas worthy of possible revision.[5]

Regardless of the outcome of the Basel II/III implementation, which is some years away in many emerging market countries, few supervisory regimes recognize movable assets in determining lending reserve requirements. This ignores the practical utility of realizing securities in movables-based financing—particularly in receivables financing done on electronic payments platforms—and discourages bankers from considering alternative movables-backed financing options.

All these inhibiting factors can be overcome. Several specialized nonbank financial institutions have entered the supply chain financing market. From Alibaba in the East, to OnDeck Capital, Kabbage, and others in the West, they are a recognized and growing presence in this area. They can ignore many of the regulatory and supervisory issues, and can adjust their business practices to minimize other obstacles, while they maximize access to the growing electronic data streams that underlie their lending models. At the same time, as nonbanks, they are constrained in many markets in fundraising, and in all markets in the range of financial products and services they can offer. Policy makers should strive to improve their enabling environments to remove barriers for banks wishing to compete in supply chain finance, particularly if they want to see longer-term financing based on supply chain relationships. Such longer-term financing will be critical to SMEs' abilities to increase productivity and efficiency (including resource and energy efficiency), which are vital to keeping up with raising quality and sustainability standards in global supply chains.

SMEs in GVCs are likely to be credit constrained for one more reason. They are likely to engage in productivity-enhancing activities and innovate. Innovation is intended in the broad sense. It includes not only evolutionary and revolutionary advances in technology, process, or product offering, but also new approaches, business models, channels, value propositions, and marketing and branding strategies, that is, the broad range of activities pursued by firms willing to find an insertion point in GVCs and upgrade their participation.

There are financial market reasons for innovation underinvestment even in the absence of externality-induced underinvestment.[6] These reasons are related to informational asymmetries (such as adverse selection and moral hazard problems) that create a gap between the private innovation rate of return and the cost of capital when the innovation investor and financier are different entities. Adverse selection occurs because banks do not know the default risk of a particular borrower; they can base the price of a loan only on the average default risk. As a result, low-risk borrowers face higher interest rates than they would if there was perfect information, and they may choose not to seek a loan.

Moral hazard emerges when banks cannot perfectly monitor the activities of the innovator after the loan has been approved. Consequently, an innovator may be tempted to take on a more risky project than what had been originally agreed, since in the case of success the innovator gets all of the upside, while in the case of failure the loss is capped. Informational asymmetries are typically a more relevant problem for start-ups and SMEs than for large companies, exacerbating the R&D underinvestment problem as is widely documented in the role that these firms play in fostering innovation (Acs and Audretsch 1987; Ewens and Fons-Rosen 2013).

In general, markets provide less finance for small and medium-size companies willing to grow and innovate than is socially desirable. As a result, start-ups and SMEs mostly use nonmarket or informal forms of financing. A survey of Japanese SMEs and start-ups (Mitsubishi UFJ Research & Consulting 2012) finds that in fewer than 25 percent of the cases funds are borrowed from private financial institutions. The founder's own funds and financing and support from family and relatives are by far the two most popular sources of capital (figure 3.9).

Most sources of financing fall in at least one of three categories of investors: (a) emotional investors, (b) strategic investors, and (c) financial investors. In the first category are those who invest out of personal emotional relationship, so investments tend to be nonmarket based. Strategic investors base their decision on some nonfinancial objective, such as access to R&D or a supplier-buyer relationship. GVC buyers or lead firms may act as strategic investors. Finally, financial investors are primarily or exclusively driven by return on investment. Market failures in financing for SMEs that can be addressed by policy intervention fall mainly in the latter category.

Figure 3.9 Support for Start-Ups and SMEs in Japan

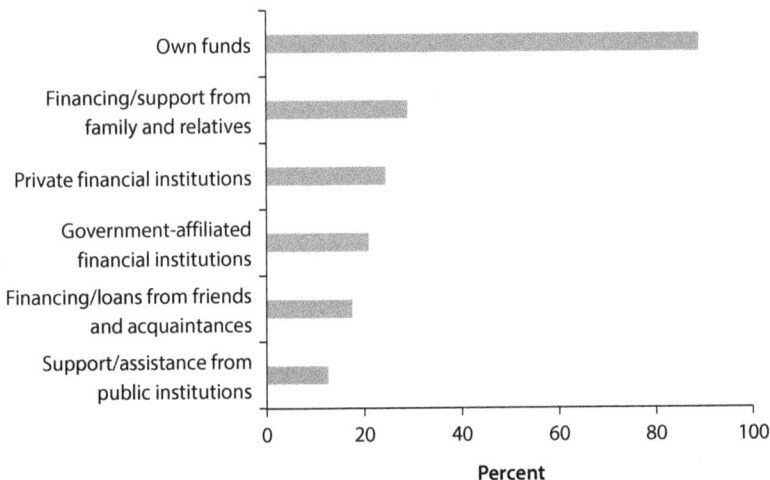

Source: Mitsubishi UFJ Research & Consulting 2012.
Note: SMEs = small and medium enterprises.

Although there are many different sources of capital (including banks, finance companies, leasing companies, public government lending programs, trade credits, private investors, venture capital, and intermediaries), the sources fall mainly into two categories: (a) debt financing, which essentially means the firms borrow money and repay with interest, and (b) equity financing, whereby the investors are rewarded with part ownership.

- Debt financing is accessible to SMEs mostly through banks after the start-up phase. As lending policies were made stricter in the wake of Basel III, banks have become more parsimonious with financing for SMEs. This is true in high-income countries (see the OECD's SME Finance Scorecard) and in low-income countries.
- Equity is another external source of finance for SMEs, and is particularly important for the more innovative SMEs. SMEs tend to prefer debt financing over equity financing, as issuing new equity dilutes an entrepreneur's control of the firm and can become a source of conflict if disagreements among shareholders emerge. Moreover, access by SMEs to equity finance is sometimes constrained by demand-side weaknesses, such as lack of "investment readiness." The latter means that SME owners are unwilling to seek external equity finance or that those who are willing to do so do not understand what equity investors are looking for and do not know how to sell their business propositions in a way that is attractive to potential investors (Mason and Kwok 2010). However, the advantages of equity financing over debt financing for SMEs are that it increases risk sharing and gives the entrepreneur access to the investors' networks and expertise.

Acting directly on the entrepreneur is only one way to support the financing of entrepreneurial activity. A common form of intervention in SME credit markets is represented by partial credit guarantee (PCG) schemes. The main objective of PCGs is to reduce the net losses that commercial banks may incur in case of default by SME borrowers. However, PCGs can potentially play a more important role, especially in countries with weak institutional environments, by improving the information available on borrowers in coordination with credit registries, and by building the credit origination and risk management capacity of participating banks. Moreover, PCGs can also play an important countercyclical role, providing support to small businesses during a downward economic cycle when a credit crunch is likely to set in.

The results from a recent survey carried out by the Italian government, in seeking to promote the internationalization of SMEs (SIMEST 2012), offer insights as to the needs for overcoming bottlenecks in the financing of GVC participation by SMEs. The ingredients of the approach suggested by the Italian agency SIMES include (a) promoting a policy that has regional connectivity, (b) connecting more than one region together (a low-income region and a high-income region), and (c) forming a public-private partnership to fix all the objectives and responsibilities that define eligibility criteria, cross-border projects, and sector coverage, entry, and exit.

Many countries have recently taken action to enhance access to equity financing, notably for young and innovative firms. Most measures are on the supply side, as these are perceived as being more direct. These range from grants, loans, and guarantee schemes, to tax incentives and equity instruments (Wilson 2015). In OECD countries, there has been an increase in the use of equity instruments, but the focus has shifted from government equity funds investing directly, to more indirect models, such as co-investment funds and funds-of-funds. These later approaches seek to leverage private investment, and several OECD countries are experimenting with different incentive structures. Although supply-side interventions have increased, there is little evidence of the impact of these instruments and whether they crowd out private investors.

The demand side is also critical for the success of seed and early-stage financing, and can include human and social capital development. Specific programs, such as incubators, accelerators, business angel networks, and matchmaking services, have become increasingly popular. Initiatives to create a more entrepreneurial culture are also vital. In many countries, the fear and cost of failure is higher than the perceived opportunities and/or the perceived skills to pursue those opportunities.

Despite these policies, the business environment in a country has perhaps the greatest impact on the provision of seed and early-stage finance. The development of financial markets and exit opportunities, whether through initial public offerings on a stock exchange or mergers and acquisitions by other firms, directly influences the development of seed and early-stage financing. Bankruptcy regulations, labor market restrictions, and other framework conditions also impact firm dynamics as well as the creation, financing, and growth of innovative firms. Regulatory barriers and administrative burdens on institutional investors, venture capital funds, angel investors, and high-growth firms can have a direct negative result on the provision of seed and early-stage finance. In particular, securities legislation and more stringent capital requirements on institutional investors could reduce the supply of investment in venture capital from banks, pension funds, and insurance companies, which have traditionally been three of the largest types of private institutional investors.

Bottlenecks in Infrastructure

Geography is an important determinant of countries' ability to join GVCs (Kowalski et al. 2015; OECD 2012). Nevertheless, the trade accessibility of countries is driven by more than the geographic distance from their trading partners. As figure 3.10 shows, major transport routes (for example, the shipping lanes depicted in light blue) effectively reduce remoteness for major urban areas with good trade and travel infrastructure. The ability of firms and countries to participate in GVCs is greatly affected by the quality of physical infrastructure, such as roads, ports, and airports, as well as the efficiency of the procedures followed in the operation of those facilities. Getting to the border is one of the most pervasive constraints to the exports of SMEs and firms in low-income countries.

Figure 3.10 Travel Time to Major Cities

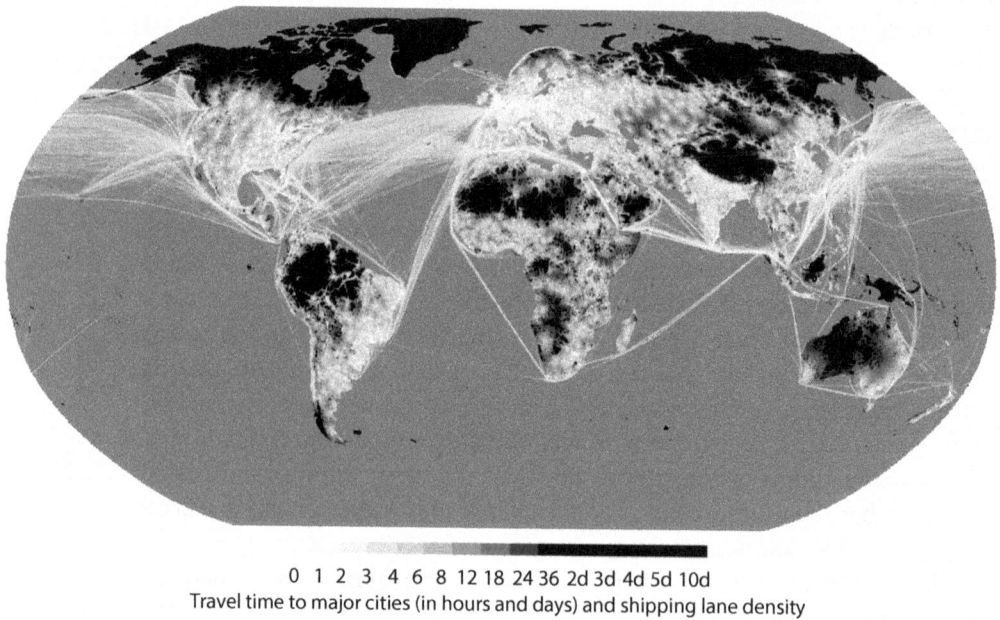

0 1 2 3   4 6 8 12 18 24 36 2d 3d 4d 5d 10d
Travel time to major cities (in hours and days) and shipping lane density

Source: Nelson 2008.
Note: The figure represents travel time to more than 8,000 cities by land, air, and water in 2000. In high-income countries, only 15 percent of people lived more than one hour from a major city; in low-income countries, the share was 65 percent.

In a world where just-in-time delivery is now the norm, and in which transit is rapid and storage is expensive, time is quite literally money. For products ranging from electronics (which can quickly become obsolete), to fruits and vegetables (which are perishable), to apparel (which is seasonal and subject to the whims of fashion), a day's delay is equivalent to a tariff of 1 percent or more. That is evidenced by the willingness of traders to pay more for faster airfreight than they do for slower water freight (Hummels, Lugovskyy, and Skiba 2007), even when shipping costs are significantly higher than tariffs or other trade costs. In their study of Africa's exports, Freund and Rocha (2010) conclude that, of all the variables responsible for delays in the production chain—transit, documentation burdens, ports, and customs delays—the most important was transit delays. Reducing inland transit time by one day would increase exports by 7 percent; such a reduction is equivalent to a 1.5 percent decrease in the tariff of all of Africa's importing trading partners. The effect is more important for time-sensitive goods, such as perishable food products.

The ability of firms and industries in low-income countries to engage in trade is determined much more by the quality of their port facilities (sea and air) than by the types of preferential access that they might enjoy in major high-income markets. Reliable and cost-competitive infrastructure facilitates trade links and FDI attraction. Significant gaps in the provision of infrastructure hold back competitiveness and the expansion of production in low-income countries. Limão and Venables (2001) estimate that transport costs for the median landlocked country are 46 percent higher than equivalent costs in countries with direct access to the coast. Similar conclusions are found in studies that measure the effects of multiple types of infrastructure together to examine the collective impact on trade. For example, Nordås and Piermartini (2004)—looking at the quality of ports, density of airports with paved railways, and density of Internet users and mobile phone subscribers—find that port infrastructure matters for all sectors, whereas timeliness and access to telecommunication matter more in the clothing and automotive sectors. Limão and Venables (2001) show that landlocked countries face higher transport costs, since their ability to trade depends on the infrastructure of the neighboring transit countries. For example, in East Africa, goods bound for landlocked countries face the time equivalent of at least three clearance processes of coastal countries. "Poor infrastructure accounts for 40% of predicted transport costs for coastal countries and up to 60% for landlocked countries." Furthermore, for landlocked countries, the authors calculate that improvements in their own infrastructure from the 25th to the 75th percentile would effectively overcome more than half the disadvantage of being landlocked (Limão and Venables 2001).

Telecommunication infrastructure is also important, not only to support value chains of physical goods, but also to enable the creation and trade of digital services, which account for a growing share of total international trade.

Infrastructure development is therefore an important element in enabling low-income countries to participate in GVCs. Whereas telecommunication links are crucial for participation in all GVCs, but notably in offshore services GVCs, transportation infrastructure and energy infrastructure play a particularly important role in manufacturing and extractive GVCs. The economies therefore need to invest more in infrastructure, but above all, they need to improve the effectiveness of public infrastructure policies.

One example of a country that successfully invested in infrastructure to reduce congestion and improve connectivity is Morocco. The country's historical port, Casablanca, remains the main port for imports and exports. The major constraint of the port is that it is located in the city, which reduces the potential for expansion and imposes additional constraints on the land transportation of goods. But ports in Morocco have seen important changes in recent years. Tanger-Med started operations in 2007 and is one of the largest regional development projects. The port container terminal had an initial capacity of 3.5 million containers and is expected to handle 8 million containers this year. The free zone of Tanger-Med is managed by the company operating the Dubai free zone, and the container terminal concessions were awarded to reputable international companies (Maersk for the first container terminal and Mediterranean Shipping Company for the second). The Moroccan government is currently planning another major port-centric development region, Nador West Med, consisting of a deep-sea port with transshipment capacity and focusing on the energy sector and a large industrial platform. The port is expected to be in service in 2019, with an initial capacity of 3 million containers, 25 million tons of hydrocarbons, and 7 million tons of coal.

Another example of how to heal the infrastructure bottlenecks constraining connectivity in low-income countries is the Indonesian Port of Jakarta. In 2008, the World Bank Group suggested ways to improve operations at Tanjung Priok, which handles two-thirds of Indonesia's international trade and has seen a rapid rise in container traffic. A main goal of the port initiative was to reduce dwell time—the average time it takes containers to clear the port. In 2011, Tanjung Priok's dwell time was six days, longer than Indonesia's regional peers (Singapore, one day; Malaysia, four days; and Thailand, five days). To reduce dwell time, the port operator raised storage fees (to discourage shippers from leaving containers for long periods) and introduced a new information technology system (to monitor and direct port traffic). A scheduled expansion of the port is expected to double its container capacity by 2017.

But building infrastructure alone without changes in policies to improve the efficiency of its use will not necessarily lead to lower transport prices. Arvis et al. (2010, p.4), using the World Bank's Logistics Performance Index (LPI), show convincingly that "logistics or trade services is more important for limiting the costs of being landlocked that investing massively in infrastructure and neglecting the functioning of logistics services." The authors point out that more than half of the time it takes to transport cargo from the port to the hinterland is spent in ports. Dwell times in Africa average more than two weeks. Those dwell times are long for several reasons: volumes are low, facilities are not operated competitively, logistics are poorly organized, storage facilities are inadequate, charges for storage are high, and port management (usually a government agency) does not have adequate incentives to speed up the process (Raballand et al. 2012). Coordination and effectiveness of public infrastructure policies are key.

For telecommunication too, the issue is not just about infrastructure, but also about access and pricing. Infrastructure—which provides the foundation for GVCs, new business models, and e-commerce—needs to be of high quality, accessible to all, and available at competitive prices. With competition in the digital economy being challenged by several major shifts, including technical convergence and the integration of business models among telecommunication providers as well as new Internet players, governments around the world must engage in efforts to protect competition, lower artificial barriers to entry, and strengthen regulatory coherence (OECD 2015b). Once infrastructure is in place, countries must implement and monitor open access policies to ensure that international connectivity routes, which often require significant investment, are provided by a sufficient number of market players.

Notwithstanding broad commitments to expand connectivity and reduce prices, some countries are still applying policies that restrict connectivity, increase prices, and reduce options for consumers. This is the case in certain African and Asian countries, such as Ghana and Pakistan. In Pakistan, for example, the government set up a cartel to set prices for incoming international calls, raising rates from US$0.02 to US$0.088. As a result, traffic fell from more than 2 billion minutes to 500 million. This in turn generated no increase in revenue, but rather resulted in a huge loss in consumer welfare. These policies contrast with those of other countries, such as India, where dramatic cuts in international termination rates, together with strong domestic competition, have seen traffic increase dramatically (figure 3.11; OECD 2015b).

Coordination between agencies in charge of infrastructure policies is essential for overcoming multiple gaps, including coverage, access, and costs. And when infrastructure projects are driven by the private sector, governments in low-income countries should seek to direct investments in such a way that domestic firms are able to reap the benefits associated with GVC participation.

Successful infrastructure building also relies on the effectiveness of public infrastructure policies. That can be problematic, as many low-income countries face resource and capacity constraints to providing high-quality infrastructure throughout the entire economy. A crucial element of success in reducing the infrastructure gap in low-income countries is good governance on infrastructure-related capital expenditures, including the quality of budgetary execution and effectiveness in negotiations for concessions.

The quality of budgetary execution reflects the extent to which actual expenditure matches intended expenditure. Poor budget implementation is a major constraint for some countries. Budgetary predictability in capital expenditure is particularly weak in Africa, Central America and the Caribbean, and South Asia. More than 30 percent of African and South Asian countries, and close to 25 percent of countries in Central America and the Caribbean, execute less than 80 percent of their budgeted capital expenditure. For instance, Angola historically underperforms in budget execution, having spent only 34 percent of its budgeted capital expenditure in 2010. In Kiribati, a least-developed country in the Pacific, budget execution in 2009 was only 20 percent. International Monetary Fund and World Bank assessments confirm that low-income countries suffer from particularly weak budget execution (Allen and Last 2007). That does not mean that infrastructure financing should not increase, but additional financing will fail to reduce infrastructure gaps unless budget execution rises. The good execution of concession contracts also matters.

Latin America's experience with concessions in the transport sector reveals a history of many and costly renegotiations. Governments have applied the model of concessions to the development of airports, roads, railways, seaports, and multimodal terminals, first in the late 1980s and early 1990s in Argentina, Chile, and Mexico, and later in Brazil, Colombia, Peru, and Central America and the Caribbean. Difficulties in the execution of concession contracts led some policy makers to question the model. In the 1990s, close to 50 percent of transport concessions were renegotiated in Argentina, Brazil, Chile, Colombia, and Mexico. In Chile, the average concession was renegotiated four times between 1993 and 2007. Nearly a quarter of investment in concessions derived from renegotiations. Today, 40 percent of existent road concession contracts have been renegotiated in Latin America. Fifty of the 60 road concessions in Chile, Colombia, and Peru

Figure 3.11 Average Termination Charges and Outgoing Minutes, 2003–12

a. Average termination charge for outgoing traffic from the United States to Africa and India

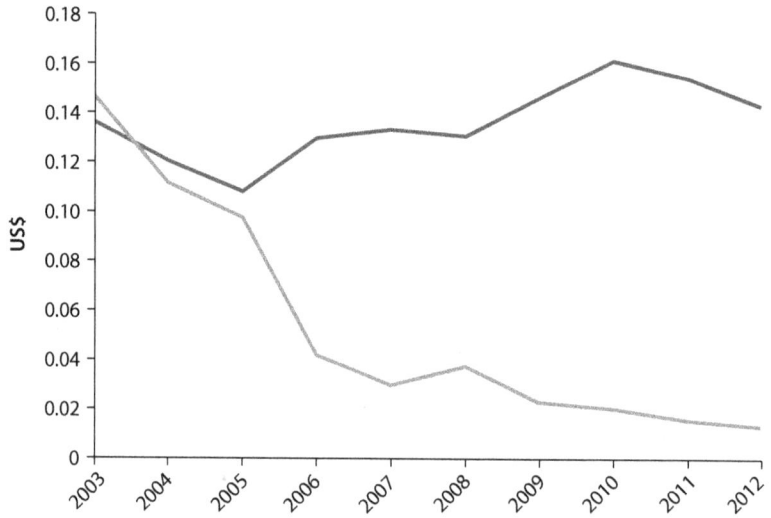

b. Outgoing minutes from U.S. carriers to Africa and India

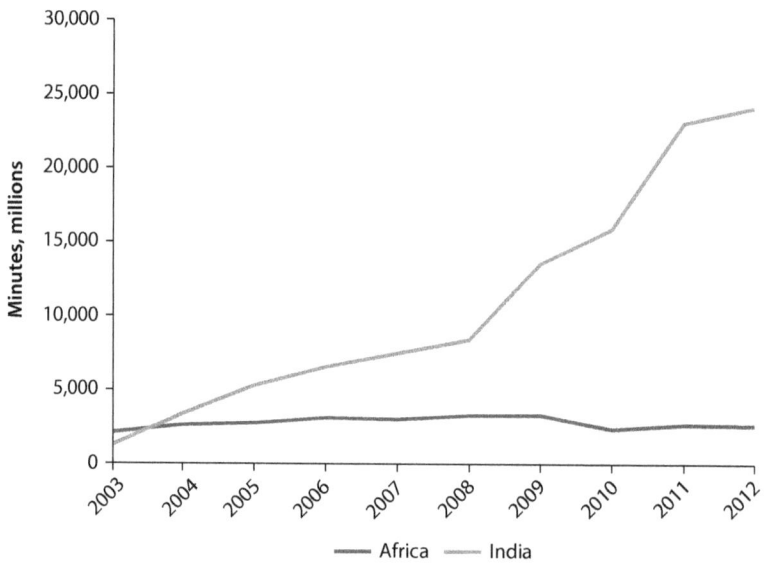

Africa — India

Source: OECD 2015b.

were renegotiated up to 2010 (Bitran, Nieto-Parra, and Robledo 2013). The additional fiscal costs amount to 50 percent of the initial value of the contracts.

Trade Logistics

Infrastructure building and well-managed infrastructure policies do not guarantee better connectivity, if they are delinked from a wider logistics strategy. Inefficient logistics raises the costs of trading and reduces the potential for trade (figures 3.12 and 3.13). For example, Morocco's LPI rank jumped from 113 in 2007 to 50 in 2012, partially reflecting that the country has implemented a comprehensive strategy to improve logistics and connectivity, and has taken advantage of its proximity to Europe. Combining border management reform with the large physical investments in the Tanger-Med Port, the strategy fostered the emergence of Morocco's just-in-time exports to Europe (especially textiles, electronics, and automotive components). Morocco's fast rise in the LPI highlights the payoffs of such a comprehensive approach. In 2011, for example, Morocco established an agency for logistics development. Banking on its location and the success of its investment in the trans-shipment port at Tanger-Med, the country is pursuing a policy to develop freight and logistics facilities and services that reach beyond its own economy—to North Africa, Southern Europe, and West Africa.

Figure 3.12 Supply Chain Bottlenecks Are the Primary Cause of Trade Costs

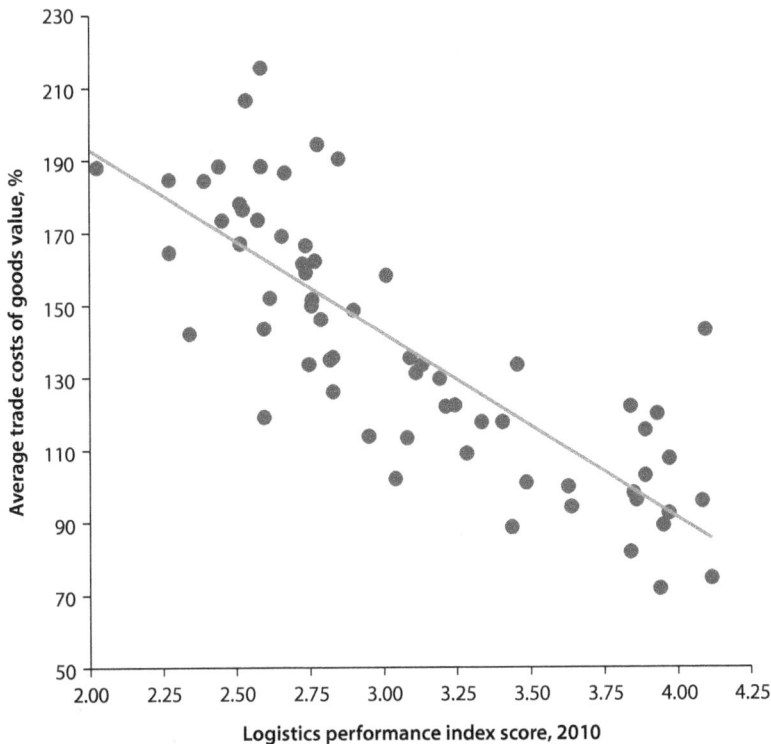

Source: World Bank, Logistics Performance Index 2010.

Figure 3.13 Logistics Performance and Connectivity

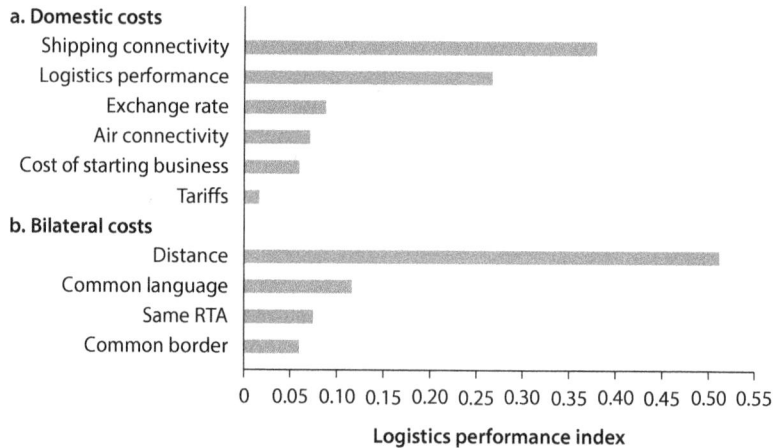

a. Domestic costs
- Shipping connectivity
- Logistics performance
- Exchange rate
- Air connectivity
- Cost of starting business
- Tariffs

b. Bilateral costs
- Distance
- Common language
- Same RTA
- Common border

Logistics performance index

Source: Arvis, Duval, et al. 2013.
Note: RTA = regional trade agreement.

Poor logistics is a major constraint to trade in low-income countries. Improving logistics performance and the efficiency of the supply chain is at the core of policies to bolster competitiveness and boost trade integration. Recent trade research shows that improving logistics is where low-income countries have the most potential to reduce trade costs. The lower the trade costs are, the more competitive, as well as globally and regionally integrated, a country is.

Bilateral trade costs capture the separation between countries or the friction in international trade networks. The costs are formally defined as the ad valorem equivalent of all factors that drive a wedge between the price of goods at the factory or farm gate in the exporting country and the price paid by a consumer in the importing country. Trade costs depend on given or intangible factors, such as geographical distance, language, and historical connections, as well as factors that can be targeted by policy interventions, such as supply chain connectivity and tariff and nontariff barriers. The United Nations Economic and Social Commission for Asia and the Pacific–World Bank bilateral trade costs database provides trade costs by country pair for manufacturing and agriculture. Arvis, Shepherd, et al. (2013) provide an estimate of the sources of trade costs. As expected, distance is a major source of trade costs, but logistics performance and connectivity are at least as important, and more so than tariffs. And as low-income countries face much higher trade costs, partly because of the importance of policy in addressing their sources, policy measures can do much to reduce them while boosting trade integration, especially through measures that improve connectivity and logistics.[7]

Exogenous determinants of trade, such as geography, are outside a country's control, but policy decisions are not. Connectivity, including logistics performance, can be addressed by a series of policy interventions. Supply chain service delivery is affected mainly by three areas: customs, infrastructure, and logistics services quality. All three constitute areas for policy regulations and should be tackled with a comprehensive approach (figure 3.14). They are important because they affect the cost incurred by firms to move goods. Logistics costs include three categories: administrative, transport, and inventory costs. Differences in logistics costs are primarily associated with the reliability of supply chains, rather than with transportation costs. Logistics costs therefore reflect logistics performance, with clear differences across countries that are driven by their efficiency in handling logistics services.

Inventory costs are the consequence of a lack of reliability of the supply chain in many low-income countries. Firms willing to enter global manufacturing value chains encounter a double penalty with extra logistics costs on inputs and exports. The causes of unreliability are rarely found in deficient physical infrastructure, but rather in inefficient clearance processes, especially at land borders and in ports, and with the performance of services available to traders, such as truck services, forwarding, or customs agents. As data from the 2007 and 2014 editions of the LPI show, overall logistics performance has improved, but some factors have moved faster than others, with the quality of logistics services rising more slowly than the quality of trade- and transport-related infrastructure and the performance of border agencies. This is especially true for low-income and lower-middle-income economies (figure 3.15).

SMEs are even more vulnerable to supply chain inefficiencies than large firms are, and SMEs typically face doubled logistics costs. The first reason is pure economics. Smaller firms have fewer economies of scale in their inventory (through a higher inventory ratio) and hence higher inventory costs, which can be punitively high in low-income countries with poor logistics performance. Size is also a disadvantage in several other respects. Small exporters tend to be more affected by a lack of transparency in clearance processes and depend more on independent services to move goods or clear them with border agencies. Logistics services may not be friendly to small shipments and services may not be available or

Figure 3.14 Firm-Level Logistics Expenditures as Percentage of Sales, 2011–12

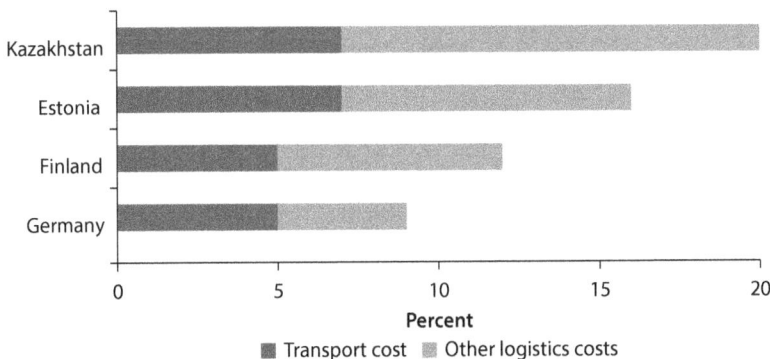

Sources: For Germany: TU Berlin; for Finland and Estonia: Turku School of Economics; for Kazakhstan: World Bank.

Figure 3.15 Percentage Change in LPI Scores, by LPI Component and Income Group, 2007–14

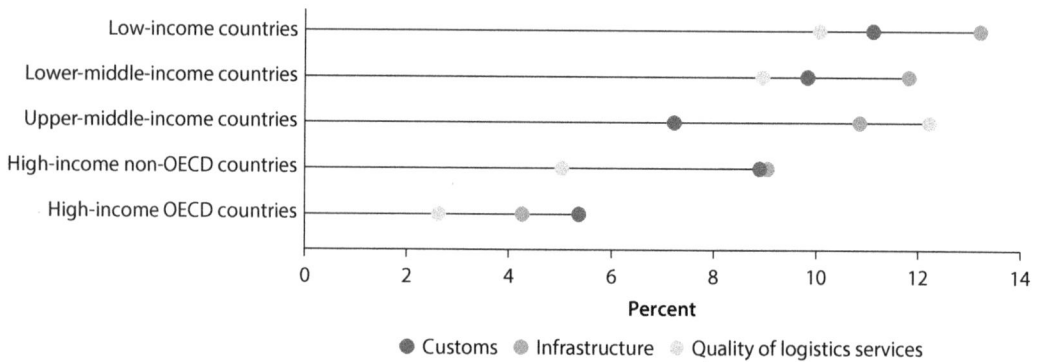

Source: World Bank Logistics Performance Index 2007, 2010, 2012, and 2014.
Note: LPI = Logistics Performance Index; OECD = Organisation for Economic Co-operation and Development.

affordable, forcing SMEs to consolidate their goods in single containers to reach their destination market. Consolidation services can be very expensive or not available at all. Nontraditional exports of fresh produce, for instance, are impossible without a cold chain and refrigerated containers. Lastly, the lack of continuity of logistics services beyond the main gateway puts SMEs in remote regions at a disadvantage to reach markets. Inter-island trade in Indonesia provides a telling example. The high cost of transporting high-quality goods, such as shrimp from eastern Indonesia to processing centers in Java, makes them too expensive to export, or similarly it is cheaper to import oranges from China than to ship them from Kalimantan to Java.

Data from a 2012 study on trends and strategies in logistics support the notion that many SMEs encounter disproportionally high logistics costs (Straube et al. 2013). Industrial firms with fewer than 250 workers on average have logistics costs of 14.7 percent of overall revenue for the business unit. In contrast, industrial firms with more than 1,000 workers reported logistics costs of only 6.7 percent of overall revenue, which was consistent with logistics costs as a share of the overall revenue reported by industrial firms with 250 to 1,000 workers (6.4 percent of overall revenue).

The survey covered 113 industrial firms in various world regions. Breaking up the results by region or country confirmed the overall results. SMEs in China reported logistics costs of 15 percent of overall revenue, while firms with more than 1,000 workers reported only 5.2 percent. For South America, the numbers were 15.3 percent for SMEs and 9.4 percent for large industrial companies with more than 1,000 workers.

Trade Facilitation

Trade facilitation enables GVC trade by reducing the time, cost, and uncertainty involved in importing and exporting. Trade facilitation improves and streamlines the processing of trade by border agencies, including customs, ministries of trade, and standards (for example, sanitary and phytosanitary standards). Trade facilitation initiatives cover a broad range of measures, from coordinating procedures and controls across border agencies under integrated border management, to the automation of customs procedures and extension to other procedures under single-window systems (box 3.2). Trade facilitation initiatives also include introducing risk management practices to reduce the incidence of physical inspection of traded goods; an authorized economic operators regime, whereby importers with a track record of compliance benefit from expedited procedures, including ex post auditing; and trade portals, where comprehensive and updated information on requirements for all products (tariff and nontariff requirements) are easily accessible.

Box 3.2 Implementing a Single-Window System in Lao PDR

Delays at customs are problematic in many low-income countries, adding to the time and unpredictability of trading and inhibiting the export competitiveness of many low-income countries as well as their participation in global value chains. One innovative approach to border processing and clearance is the establishment of national single-window systems. Such systems allow traders to submit all the information required by regulatory agencies through a single electronic gateway, instead of submitting separate information to multiple government entities using a variety of paper, electronic, or other interfaces.

Establishing a single window involves significant challenges and complexity, requiring the cooperation of multiple government agencies, many of which must engage in significant institutional reforms. Recent World Bank experience suggests that several preconditions are needed to launch a single-window program, including (a) the building of a strong business case, (b) careful assessment of risks and capabilities, (c) a strong government mandate supported by political will and stakeholder buy-in, (d) agreement among government agencies on the structure of governance and leadership, and (e) a work program with key milestones linked to appropriate resources and accountability for all participants.

Given government commitment, even the poorest countries can make progress in this area. A good example is the World Bank Group's work in the Lao People's Democratic Republic. With support provided by the World Bank and others, the government developed a National Trade Facilitation Strategy and established a National Trade Facilitation Secretariat to provide for the implementation of the strategy. With support from the World Bank, Lao PDR has established a Trade Information Portal that allows traders to access all relevant trade rules, regulations, procedures, fee schedules, and forms from all border management agencies through a single user-friendly website. The Trade Information Portal is an important first step in establishing a full electronic single-window system.

The World Bank Group is currently engaged in a preparatory project to support Lao PDR in making informed decisions going forward with the single-window system. This project includes technical support on legal and regulatory frameworks, fee models, and governance structures, as well as development of a comprehensive capacity-building and transition strategy.

Source: McLinden 2013.

Trade facilitation matters for small businesses more than for large companies, since costs are fixed regardless of a firm's size or revenue. Integrating SMEs and firms in low-income countries into value chains requires addressing their two main sources of disadvantage: (a) lack of economies of scale, and (b) excessive bureaucracy, uncertainty, and lack of transparency in trade-related procedures.

SMEs often face higher obstacles to engage in international trade than large enterprises do. For this reason, SMEs are often forced to confine their business activities to the geographical area close to their production site. Difficulties in exporting stem—at least partly—from the high costs of transporting their small shipments and from greater bureaucracy.

Of all the trade facilitation measures, key initiatives to level the playing field for SMEs include tackling information failures, improving the effectiveness of clearance processes, and introducing initiatives for creating awareness around key constraints.

- Delays in passing through customs have often been singled out as the villain in border delays. In fact, more often than not, it is the combination of other agencies—health, agriculture, quarantine, police, immigration, and standards—that causes systematically worse rankings in the World Bank's LPI. Non-customs agencies are concerned more about their parochial risk management objectives than about speeding goods across the border; they frequently lack the reform blueprints and technical guidelines built from international experience to implement the reforms that are found in the customs world. They have not embraced automation or risk-based management systems that have allowed many customs agencies to speed their processing times and improve reliability.
- Despite reforms in many customs agencies, the facilitated procedures are naturally geared toward larger firms. For example, having small flows and fewer operations, SMEs face difficulties in accessing fast-track programs like authorized economic operator programs. Although SMEs can benefit from working with logistics operators that have those regimes in place, SMEs nevertheless remain disadvantaged.

Hence, SMEs will benefit even more than large companies from measures facilitating the clearance of goods or improving logistics services. Reducing the asymmetry of information vis-à-vis public operators will increase transparency in clearance processes. Other measures, including automation, single windows, and trade portals will facilitate information, speed up border procedures, and reduce costs. And better coordination and cooperation between public agencies will reduce coordination costs for the firm. Public-private dialogue initiatives are also important, as they too contribute to improving access to information and creating awareness within nationwide trade facilitation initiatives, thereby helping to bring down the cost of trading across borders for SMEs.

The principles of successful trade facilitation are well documented and have recently been codified in the WTO Agreement on Trade Facilitation (box 3.3). Implementation of that agreement will contribute to addressing some of the bottlenecks.

Other, less traditional, initiatives help too. There are positive experiences of collective actions and innovative solutions to counterbalance the lack of economies of scale in logistics. A successful example of trade facilitation measures helping SMEs participate in trade value chains by reaching international markets is the export of fresh mangoes from Mali to Europe. The export program, supported by international donors, was able to overcome several challenges, including transport and logistics problems, lack of market information and investment at the production level, and a non-conducive regulatory environment for exporters. By designing interventions along the whole value chain, including harvest and transport, Malian exporters were able to access the market in Europe, benefiting small-scale growers in Mali (Sangho, Labaste, and Ravry 2010).

Another successful example is the Exporta Fácil program in Brazil, Colombia, Peru, and Uruguay (box 3.4). These programs bear important lessons. For SMEs, costs and administrative burdens are the main impediments to trade. Cutting them is thus key. Using large physical networks to implement the reform is necessary to achieve success. Improvements in the producing country must be

---

Box 3.3 WTO Agreement on Trade Facilitation

After more than nine years of negotiations, World Trade Organization (WTO) members reached consensus on a Trade Facilitation Agreement at the Ministerial Conference held in Bali, Indonesia, on December 7, 2013. The final agreement builds on the now 50-year-old trade rules covered by Articles V, VIII, and X of the General Agreement on Tariffs and Trade, and contains provisions for faster and more efficient customs and border management procedures. The key measures include commitments on publishing and making available information for traders, as well as adopting modern approaches to customs and border management. The principles include the following:

- Operational standards by customs agencies for risk management for post-audit clearance
- Transparency measures, such as transparency of new legislation, appeals against administrative decisions, and advance rulings
- Improved cooperation between government agencies, such as in implementing national single-window systems
- Guidelines for streamlining international transit procedures.

The new agreement brings many of the standards and best practices enshrined in other international instruments under the formal auspices of the WTO. In many respects, the Bali agreement spells out only minimum common standards. The full benefits of trade facilitation will be fully realized only if countries are prepared to go beyond it, for example, with regionally integrated facilitation frameworks similar to those of the European Union.

matched by efforts in destination and transit countries, and all stakeholders in the supply chain need to be involved in the implementation of the reform, since capacity development by targeting only exporting SMEs is not sufficient. More generally, export processes should address all three dimensions of the export business: (a) physical handling of export items, (b) data exchange and processing, and (c) facilitation of financial transactions.

Box 3.4 The Exporta Fácil Program in Latin America

The Exporta Fácil program in Brazil, Colombia, Peru, and Uruguay was based on an initiative of Brazil's public postal operator in the early 2000s, which continued a series of measures by the Brazilian government aimed at fostering exports by small and medium enterprises (SMEs). Using the postal network's 8,000 outlets, SMEs could export goods at much lower cost and with less bureaucracy than before. Thanks to cooperation between the government, the postal service, and customs, the number of documents needed to dispatch parcels under 30 kilograms with a value of less than US$10,000 (later raised to US$50,000) was vastly reduced. The postal service also acted as a precursor of a single-window system, removing the need for SME exporters to interact separately with customs, health, and environment agencies; export agencies; and others.

The Brazil initiative was successful in raising SME exports and had demonstration effects. The Initiative for the Integration of Regional Infrastructure in South America (IIRSA) designed a similar project for Colombia, Ecuador, Peru, and Uruguay in 2007. The explicit purpose was to enhance SME competitiveness in IIRSA member states so that they could access regional and international markets. Cost savings during the export-import process for SMEs were achieved not just through the low cost of the designated operator (the postal service), they were achieved also because costs previously associated with trade disappeared, for example, exporters' trips to major cities, contracting of customs officers or foreign trade specialists, training, and certificates of origin. The cost of the pilot program in the four countries was US$2.7 million.

The results for export volume have been very positive: in Brazil, export volumes using the Exporta Fácil program grew from US$160,000 in 1999 to around US$250 million in 2010. In Peru, export volumes using the program grew from US$72,500 in 2007 (third quarter only) to US$718,000 in 2010 (third quarter only). In Brazil, Exporta Fácil raised SMEs' competitiveness and facilitated their access to international trade. A greater variety of Brazilian products was exported to more destinations. Using the service, between 2002 and 2008, overall about 10,000 businesses that had never exported before were able to engage in international trade. One in 10 Brazilian exporters would have been unable to export without the program in 2005. The service proved to be particularly suited to the objectives of international development, as economic analysis showed that it was more widely used in poorer, less service-oriented communities.

Several lessons were learned from the Exporta Fácil program. First, for SMEs, costs and administrative burdens are the main impediments to trade. Cutting them is thus key.

box continues next page

Box 3.4 The Exporta Fácil Program in Latin America *(continued)*

Using the postal service as a customs broker can help with both. Second, a large physical net-work such as the international post (660,000 branches worldwide) is required. Third, easy export solutions at the national level must be complemented by similar efforts in destination and transit countries to ensure effectiveness. Fourth, a joint effort by all stakeholders and covering all actors in the supply chain is required, including coordination within the govern-ment. Capacity development targeting only exporting SMEs is not sufficient. The customs administration and logistics companies should also be supported to provide easy and effec-tive solutions. Fifth, easy export processes should address all three dimensions of the export business: (a) physical handling of export items, (b) data exchange and processing, and (c) facilitation of financial transactions.

Trade Policy

Trade policy per se may figure less prominently in the GVC-led global economy than it did in past generations, but nonetheless it remains a critical part of the policy mix. The way that trade policy is conceived, however, requires some reor-dering. Policy makers must now give as much consideration to imports as they traditionally have to exports, and they must value time as much as tariffs (OECD 2013b). This chapter has clearly indicated that time is a priority, since participa-tion in geographically fragmented GVCs frequently requires quick and inexpen-sive movement of goods over borders, and delays in those movements can be deadly to the aspirations for upgrading and strengthening the GVC participation of an economy.

Reducing import tariffs and export procedures should be a priority for com-petitively engaging in GVCs, and one does not substitute for the other. Tariffs are an additional cost imposed on imports. Not surprisingly, countries in South Asia, which have high average import tariffs compared with the global average, also post low integration rates in manufacturing GVCs, compared with countries from Southeast Asia that are well integrated in GVCs (figure 3.16). For example, Pakistan has an average tariff 300 percent higher than the average tariff prevalent in some countries in the Gulf Cooperation Council, Latin America, and Southeast Asia, and highly distortionary ad hoc regulations or statutory regula-tory orders. Pakistan is one of the countries that are least integrated in GVCs, despite a good manufacturing base and the ability of Pakistani firms to produce and export world-class products, such as the high-end Laguiole knives, and the Adidas Brazuca, the official football for the 2014 World Cup as well as for the national championships of countries such as Argentina, Colombia, Germany, Paraguay, Portugal, the Republic of Korea, and República Bolivariana de Venezuela.

Tariffs on inputs are particularly costly because they are used directly in production and drive up costs. Tariffs on inputs not only affect the competitive-ness of domestic producers, they also affect their ability to participate in GVCs (OECD, WTO, and UNCTAD 2013; OECD, WTO, and World Bank 2014).

Figure 3.16 Simple Average Tariffs, Selected Countries, 2014

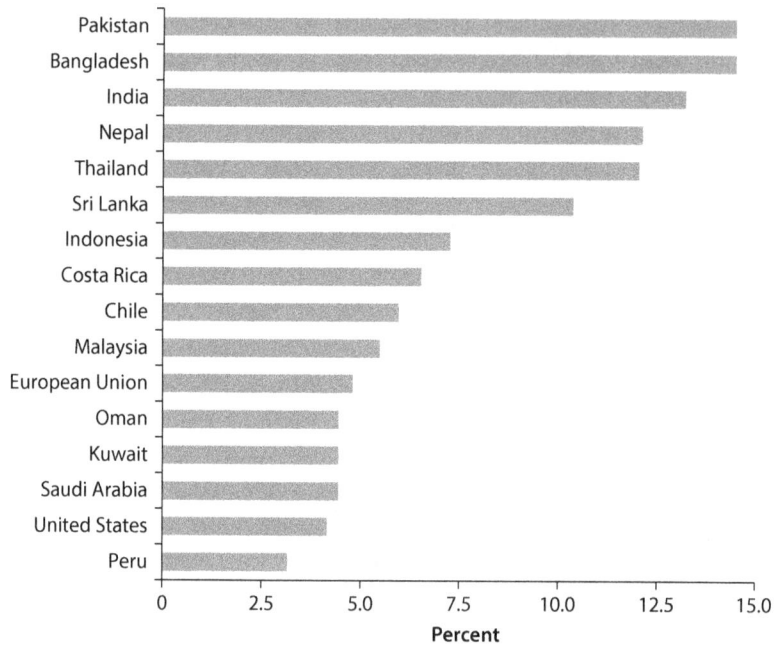

Source: World Bank computations, using World Integrated Trade Solution and national information sources.

The intricate structure of GVCs can multiply the effects of even nuisance-level duty rates (figure 3.17). In one example, a disk drive is assembled in Thailand, which acts as a hub for a supply network involving 43 components from 10 other countries and 10 components produced in Thailand (Baldwin 2006; Hiratsuka 2005). The disk drive is then sent to China, which serves as a similar hub for the assembly of a laptop computer, which is finally sent to the United States.

Koopman et al. (2010) calculate so-called tariff magnification ratios for manufacturing products and show that taking into account tariffs along all stages of the supply chain significantly raises effective tariff protection.[8] Empirical evidence shows that this magnification effect is particularly important in sectors characterized by long value chains with several production stages, such as communication and electronics, motor vehicles, basic metals, and textiles. Driven by such mechanisms, cross-country studies of the effects of tariffs on growth of gross domestic product consistently find that higher tariffs in general are associated with lower growth rates, and tariffs on intermediate inputs are particularly important. For example, Estevadeordal and Taylor (2009) find strong evidence that liberalizing tariffs on imported capital and intermediate goods raises growth rates by about 1 percentage point annually in the liberalizing countries, whereas the effects of reducing tariffs on final goods are less important.

Research highlights the adverse effect of intermediate input tariffs on industry structure and trade. For instance, a recent OECD study (Johansson and

Figure 3.17 Tariffs on the Gross Value and the Domestic Value Added of Exports, 2009

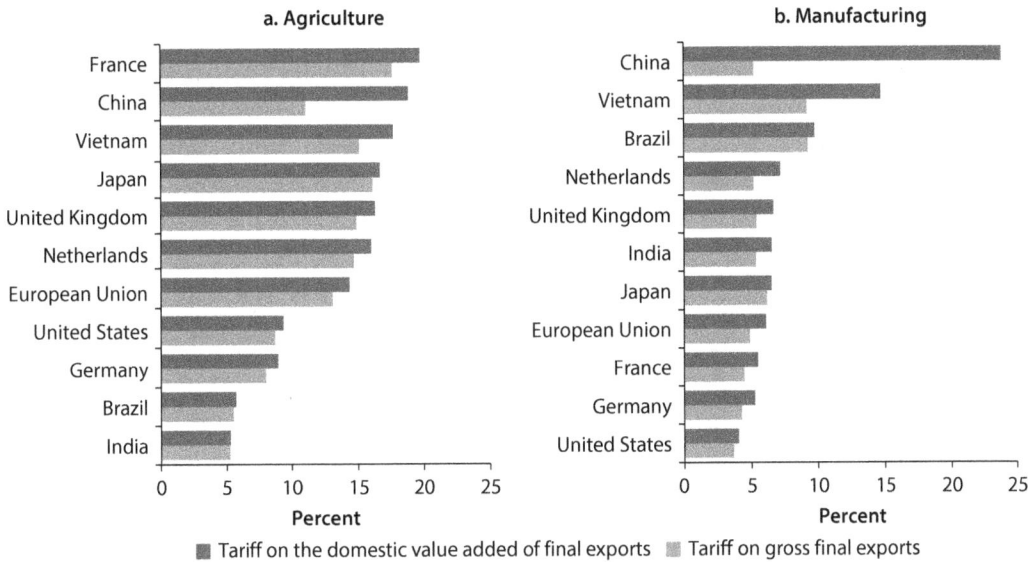

a. Agriculture

b. Manufacturing

■ Tariff on the domestic value added of final exports   ■ Tariff on gross final exports

Source: OECD, WTO, and UNCTAD 2013.
Note: Values are applied average tariffs, weighted by the share of each sector and destination market in the country's agricultural or manufacturing exports. For European Union countries, tariffs are calculated on extra-European Union exports.

Olaberría 2014) suggests that if tariffs on electronics were to be reduced in a country where such tariffs are high (for example, Brazil) to the median level in the sample of countries included in the analysis, exports of electronics could increase by 26 percent. Furthermore, intermediate input tariffs not only affect exports in the same industry, they also have a sizable negative effect on exports of downstream industries (OECD, WTO, and World Bank 2014). For instance, if a country with high tariffs on textiles (for example, South Africa) were to reduce them to the median level in the sample of countries included in the analysis, exports of clothing from this country, whose inputs embed more than 40 percent of textile products, could increase by more than 30 percent.[9]

Some actions that countries take to facilitate the import of inputs are much less comprehensive and effective than the elimination of tariffs through either multilateral or regional agreements. They may, for example, offer special treatment to imports in competitive spaces, special economic zones (SEZs), or related programs, which can take on a variety of forms. Examples include *maquiladoras* in much of Latin America and foreign trade zones in China and the United States. Within the framework of GVCs, SEZs and other competitive spaces have a clear rationale, but empirical research also shows that they deliver mixed results. Creating SEZs can help attract GVC activities that are highly responsive to tariffs, and thus may feature as a strategy for insertion. However, there is a risk that SEZs may remain isolated pockets of production, and that host countries may become too vulnerable to changes in the strategies of MNEs. SEZs do not necessarily help create the spillovers and links that facilitate upgrading among domestic firms if participating firms engage in little more than processing activities.

MNEs that locate facilities within SEZs may do so as part of a cost-reduction strategy, and may therefore be less likely than domestic firms to prioritize functional upgrading or R&D investments. Once wages and costs in the host country increase above a certain threshold, those activities may move to an economy that offers lower costs, as MNEs have become increasingly footloose. Furthermore, SEZs or duty drawback systems do not allow second-tier domestic suppliers to join GVCs. High and escalating tariffs act as a kind of "currency overvaluation," pricing out domestic suppliers. The risk is particularly acute for small economies where access to the domestic market or local knowledge is of limited importance to the location decisions of MNEs. Responding to this risk requires combining integration in GVCs with strengthening domestic capabilities to enhance productivity and innovation.

Nontariff measures (NTMs) raise specific concerns for GVC participation (OECD 2013c). NTMs consist of any policies (other than ordinary customs tariffs) that influence trade flows, and they can block the efficient operation of supply chains. Although NTMs should not have protectionist intent, they nevertheless can have an impact on trade costs that is of a much larger magnitude than the impact of tariffs (figure 3.18).

Focusing on NTMs in G20 economies (OECD 2011a) finds that the trade cost impact of NTMs is more important than prevailing tariff rates in obstructing trade. That is true even in the more sensitive, and hence tariff-protected, industrial sectors, such as motor vehicles and processed foods. Most NTMs are put in place to ensure that imported products comply with the same standards and regulations as domestic products. Trade costs and trade frictions arise from

Figure 3.18 Average Level of Restrictiveness Imposed on Imports

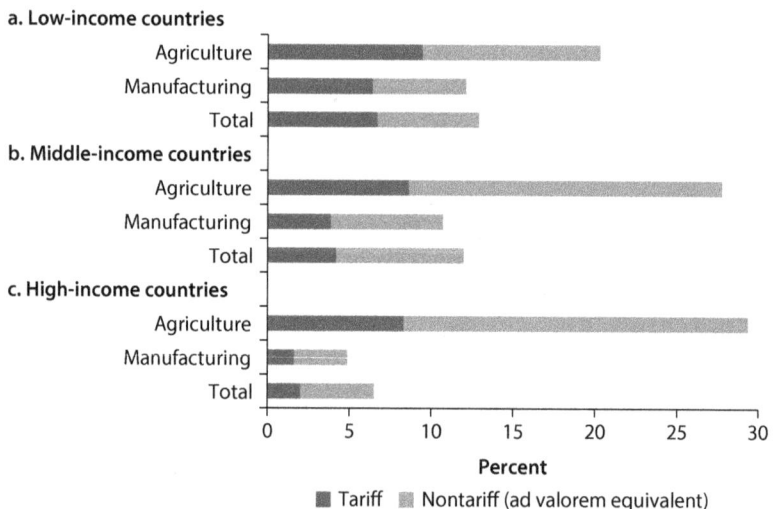

a. Low-income countries
b. Middle-income countries
c. High-income countries

Percent

■ Tariff ▦ Nontariff (ad valorem equivalent)

Source: OECD, WTO, World Bank Group 2014.

differences in regulations and their implementation, and obviously a "reduction to zero" is not a feasible option for those NTMs; a certain amount of trade costs related to those measures will always exist. Hence, in the OECD (2011a), the focus is on the portion of NTM-related trade costs that is actually "reducible," and finds significant positive overall income and employment effects of reducing them. The highest potential gains are observed when countries engage in their own reforms, including in low-income countries in Africa and Asia, which underscores the importance of domestic policy reforms for tapping into the potential of GVCs.

One form of trade barrier that appears to be on the rise is local content requirements (LCRs) (Stone, Messent, and Flaig 2015). LCRs have been used in several cases by governments that have established domestic policies supporting the generation of electricity from renewable energy, especially wind energy and solar photovoltaic (PV) energy, leading to several high-profile trade disputes (box 3.5). In the context of GVCs, policy measures aimed at protecting domestic solar PV and wind turbine manufacturers may hinder downstream investment in renewable energy–based power generation by raising the cost of inputs, which can result in increased installation costs and reduced demand for renewable energy. That in turn could lead to suboptimal levels of international and domestic investment throughout the solar PV and wind energy GVCs, while increasing investment risk by raising the prospects of trade disputes.

Box 3.5 Trade and Investment Barriers: The Case of LCRs Affecting Renewable Energy

Trade and investment barriers are particularly challenging in renewable energy, as they may hamper the optimization of emerging global value chains (GVCs) in the production of solar photovoltaic (PV) energy and wind energy. The manufacture of solar PV panels, wind turbines, and intermediate components is increasingly spread across countries and integrated within GVCs, accounting for a growing share of international trade of intermediate products (especially solar PV panels).

Over the past decade, governments from high-income countries and emerging economies have provided substantial support to solar PV and wind energy that has been crucial in stimulating domestic and international investment. Since 2008, however, the perceived potential of green energy to serve as a lever for growth and employment has led several governments, in a post-crisis recovery context, to design incentive measures aimed at (a) supporting domestic solar PV and wind turbine manufacturers, notably through granting preferential access to financing (for example, through low-cost loans or loan guarantees); (b) improving the export performance of solar PV and wind energy component manufacturers through targeted measures; (c) encouraging domestic and foreign firms to purchase solar or wind turbine equipment manufactured locally (for example, by imposing local content requirements [LCRs] as a precondition for benefiting from a feed-in tariff or to win a public tender); or (d) restricting imports (for example, through tariffs).

box continues next page

Box 3.5 Trade and Investment Barriers: The Case of LCRs Affecting Renewable Energy *(continued)*

The majority of those measures aim at developing a domestic manufacturing base in solar and wind energy or protecting domestic manufacturers against the alleged use of trade-distorting subsidies by countries seeking to support their own exporting producers. Research by the Organisation for Economic Co-operation and Development (OECD) shows that LCRs for solar or wind energy have been planned or implemented at the national or subnational level in at least 15 high-income countries and emerging economies, for the most part since 2008. Several countries have also used direct financial transfers and tax credits to provide preferential access to finance for domestic solar PV or wind turbine producers. Other policy impediments to international trade and investment exist, such as limits on foreign ownership, but remain relatively limited in OECD countries. More research is needed to assess the importance of technical barriers to trade (for example, divergent standards) and operational obstacles (for example, preferential access to the grid or land).

The widespread use of LCRs in solar and wind energy has resulted in several World Trade Organization disputes—five of the 63 World Trade Organization disputes since September 2010. The alleged use of dumping or harmful subsidies has resulted in an escalation of domestic trade remedies involving solar PV and wind energy. Since 2012, several large high-income and emerging economies have launched investigations into alleged dumping and subsidizing, leading to the imposition of anti-dumping duties, countervailing duties, or both, on a variety of products associated with solar PV and wind energy.

Sources: Stone, Messent, and Flaig 2015 and the chronological list of dispute cases on the World Trade Organization's website at http://www.wto.org/english/tratop_e/dispu_e/dispu_status_e.htm.

The issues affecting trade in services are similar to, but in some ways distinct from, those affecting trade in goods. Restrictions on market access to services in the international marketplace can have a direct impact on manufacturing, agriculture, and mining. That is particularly true for services that act as essential enablers in the geographic dispersion of GVCs. Such services include information and communication technology (ICT), which reduces the cost of coordination for GVCs and is an important enabler of trade in services; supply chain management services (to reduce inventories, shorten lead times, and enable faster customer response); and improved logistics services, including real-time monitoring of physical assets worldwide through the "Internet of Things" (OECD 2015b). High-quality professional, technical, and financial services also enable GVCs and help firms create value in GVCs through differentiation and customization (USITC 2013a, 2013b). The quality of services supporting GVCs in a given country depends not only on market access for qualified foreign providers, but also a robust national education system to train local entrants.

The openness of national markets to foreign services providers varies widely across countries.[10] There are significant restrictions on entry, ownership, and operations, and licensing procedures remain highly discretionary in many countries. In all countries, professional and transportation services are among the most protected industries, whereas retail, telecommunication, and even finance tend to be more open. Nonetheless, there are significant niches for low-income countries to provide services in support of GVCs. After the Great Recession of 2008–09, cost pressures on multinationals led to increased outsourcing of business processes, knowledge processes, and information technology to low-income countries (Gereffi and Fernandez-Stark 2010).

Certification and Compliance with International Standards

Sustainable management of GVCs has become an area of increased focus for companies because of competitive pressures triggered by increasing demands for quality and product certification, as well as for sustainable use of resources and sustainable environmental, labor, and social conditions of production. Consumers around the world increasingly demand products and services that are simultaneously good for the economy, the environment, and society—the triple bottom line of sustainable growth.

Incorporating sustainability standards into GVCs has become critical for companies to meet several objectives, (a) ensuring minimum standards in management practices, including in such areas as the health and safety of workers and minimum working age; (b) reducing business costs while maintaining the sustainability of business operations; and (c) sourcing materials that are environmentally and socially sustainable. These trends are therefore leading many companies to incorporate environmental, social, and governance requirements based on sustainability standards in contractual relationships with local suppliers. Suppliers that are able to meet those standards are more likely to enjoy increased demand and competitive pricing for their products.

The rising number of quality and safety standards is, in part, driven by concerns about information, coordination, and traceability, which are more acute in a world dominated by GVCs. For firms in low-income countries, meeting the standards of global buyers and lead firms is often a necessary condition for being competitive. Compliance with sanitary and phytosanitary regulations is important, for example, for being competitive in agricultural trade. Low-income countries have more than tripled their exports of high value-added foods—fruits and vegetables, fish, meats, and spices—since 1980 (Jaffee 2006).

Far more inhibiting than border rejections for international trade are the myriad of measures that preclude producers' countries from entering global markets. Disdier, Fontagne, and Mimouni (2008) find that technical regulations in agricultural trade significantly retard trade in some subsectors, but at the same time, well-designed regulations and conformity assessment procedures can facilitate trade (van Tongeren, Beghin, and Marette 2009; van Tongeren et al. 2010). Standards can also facilitate trade if they can provide information to potential suppliers and overcome problems of informational asymmetry that would otherwise stifle exports.

One of the most important issues is about assessing the costs of complying with international standards as compared with the opportunity cost of serving regional markets. This is the case because adopting higher standards involves greater difficulties and challenges for SMEs and low-income countries than for larger firms and high-income countries. Increases in production and trade costs can originate from the required compliance with a multitude of standards and technical regulations. For this reason, Cadot and Malouche (2012) suggest that sequencing may be important. They suggest that low-income countries and SMEs may first need to expand into the regional market to gain scale and learning economies and then adopt stringent international standards. Jensen and Keyser (2012) further argue that international standards would be counterproductive if they were applied to milk products in the East African Community where small-scale producers account for the bulk of production; they argue that a better strategy is for each country to apply its own standards, work toward establishing mutual recognition to spur trade, and progressively improve regional standards as the industry reaches scale and consumers demand higher quality.

The costs for SMEs and firms in low-income countries arise from the complexity and heterogeneity of international standards. Private firms in GVCs—whether as part of intra-firm trade, captive suppliers, or modular trade—increasingly set and transmit information about private standards, enforce their application as a condition of purchase, and often have a role in their formulation. Firms in countries seeking to enter foreign markets will have an advantage if they can affiliate with a GVC with native leadership in that foreign market. Nevertheless, in the most tightly controlled GVCs, standards constitute an important barrier to new competition that can be surmounted only through affiliation with a competing chain.

Moreover, the multiplication of environmental and social sustainability standards can also pose a barrier to entry to GVC participation by SMEs, even in those cases in which standards are voluntary in the country of end-product retail. The voluntary adoption of such standards by retailers with a major market share applies a de facto obligation up the supply chain (for example, Walmart's commitment to sell 100 percent Marine Stewardship Council–certified fish products).

To complicate matters further, private standard setting has gone beyond specifications for products to include production processes—often as firms have had to respond to consumers' concerns about labor conditions in factories. Brand name companies have found themselves susceptible to considerable reputational risk unless they ensure that their suppliers provide decent working conditions. For example, consumer protests led Nike to establish the Nike Code of Conduct, aimed at improving its contract factories. By 2005, the company disclosed its entire list of suppliers, and in 2007, it made public its auditing tools (Mayer and Pickles 2010). More recently, Apple found itself under criticism for poor working conditions at Foxconn in China, one of the country's largest employers and a sole supplier of iPads. Apple took swift action to address the critiques, and Foxconn changed many of its practices governing overtime work and wages (see Fair Labor Association 2012).

Those experiences and several studies point to the fact that private standards have been most effective when a lead firm with a differentiated consumer product can exert power over its supply chain (Mayer and Gereffi 2010).

The World Bank Group's experience in supporting low-income countries (for example, Bangladesh and Cambodia) to comply with standards suggests that a holistic approach, which is country focused and sustained over time, is necessary (box 3.6).

At the international level, the convergence of public and private voluntary standards, through national or international guidelines, could help. Upstream firms supplying components to several destinations may have to duplicate production processes to comply with conflicting standards, or incur burdensome certification procedures multiple times for the same product. In food value chains, process standards adapted to one country's requirements may render exporting to another country infeasible. Promoting the convergence of standards and certification requirements and encouraging mutual recognition agreements would go a long way toward alleviating the burden of compliance and enhancing the competitiveness of small-scale exporters. That is true for environmental and social sustainability standards as well as for quality and safety standards.

Conditions That Enable SMEs to Reach Scale

A range of external framework conditions also affects the capacity of SMEs to participate in GVCs, by affecting their ability to reach a sufficient minimum scale. SMEs often face higher obstacles to engage in international trade than large enterprises do; and for this reason SMEs are often forced to conduct their

---

Box 3.6 World Bank Group's Engagement in Bangladesh

The World Bank and the International Finance Corporation have been engaged with Bangladesh on improving social, labor, and environmental performance in the textile sector since 2005. The experience gathered over the past few years has reaffirmed the importance of having a broad program based on several targeted interventions. The World Bank Group's approach has been based on driving reform through five key actions: (a) engaging at the firm level, (b) strengthening the services market (supplier base), (c) improving infrastructure, (d) improving the business environment, and (e) creating platforms for public-private dialogue.

Specific interventions have included, for example, the Partnership for Cleaner Textiles, the Textile Competitiveness Project, and multiple initiatives focused on environmental and social issues in special economic zones. Each of those projects harnessed the World Bank Group's expertise across several areas, especially in developing stakeholder engagement and fostering public-private collaboration. As a result, progress has been made, and demonstration effects are becoming visible within and across global value chains. Bangladesh thus offers important lessons to other producer countries on the challenges of reform, including (a) how to encourage and incentivize firms to join initiatives and take action, (b) how to nurture domestic service providers, (c) how to develop capacity in banks to provide greater access to finance, (d) how to design projects with social inclusivity at their core, and (e) how to create mechanisms to sustain reform over the longer term.

---

business activities in a geographical area close to their production site. Restrictions on labor mobility and immigration constraints are among the factors that affect the ability of entrepreneurs to enter international markets, scale up their production, and exploit economies of scale. Although there are some programs at the bilateral or regional level to facilitate entrepreneurs' mobility internationally, there are no such schemes at the global level.

Examples of ongoing initiatives include the Asia-Pacific Economic Cooperation (APEC) Business Travel Card (ABTC), which provides fast and efficient travel for business people within the APEC region, contributing to APEC's goal of free and open trade and investment. According to the APEC Policy Support Unit study on "The Impact of Business Mobility in Reducing Trade Transaction Costs in APEC," the ABTC scheme reduced transaction costs for ABTC holders by 38 percent between March-July 2010 and March-July 2011, representing a total savings of US$3.7 million (APEC Policy Support Unit 2011).[11] The total at-the-border immigration time savings experienced by ABTC holders for the period was 62,413 hours, corresponding to a monetary value of US$1.9 million. Another initiative is the U.K. program that allows non–European Union entrepreneurs, who show the ability to invest at least £200,000 and have a business plan to create at least two jobs, to obtain a temporary visa. In addition, several Canadian provinces have launched programs to attract foreign investors who are willing to invest substantial sums of money to create a new business, similar to the U.S. Immigrant Investor visa program.

Another area where policy matters concerns firm entry. Lower entry barriers for new SMEs imply that new entrants can start at a smaller size, as they have more room for experimentation. For example, administrative burdens (red tape) and product market regulations can serve as barriers to entry and entrepreneurship, limiting the entry of young SMEs and restricting competition in the market. In addition, access to finance and capital market failures may particularly affect entrants and young firms, and will also affect the future growth of firms through a less efficient selection of firms at entry (Andrews and Cingano 2014). Although barriers to entrepreneurship have been lowered in many G20 countries over the past decade, they remain relatively high in several countries (figure 3.19; OECD 2015a).

Recent work at the OECD shows that in many OECD and emerging economies, young SMEs (that is, start-ups) do not reach a sufficient scale. Figure 3.20 shows differences across countries to the extent that young firms grow after their entry in the market. Although there are some differences across countries in the size of start-ups at entry, those differences are not particularly striking. The situation is markedly different when considering older businesses. For instance, on average, an older manufacturing business in France is half the size of one in the United States, although start-ups in France are larger than those in the United States. In some countries, such as Italy and Japan, there is only a small difference between the size of start-ups and that of mature firms.

Policies that affect firm exit matter too, because they limit the ability of entrepreneurial firms to wind down their activities and start again. Subsidies to

Figure 3.19 Barriers to Entrepreneurship, 2013

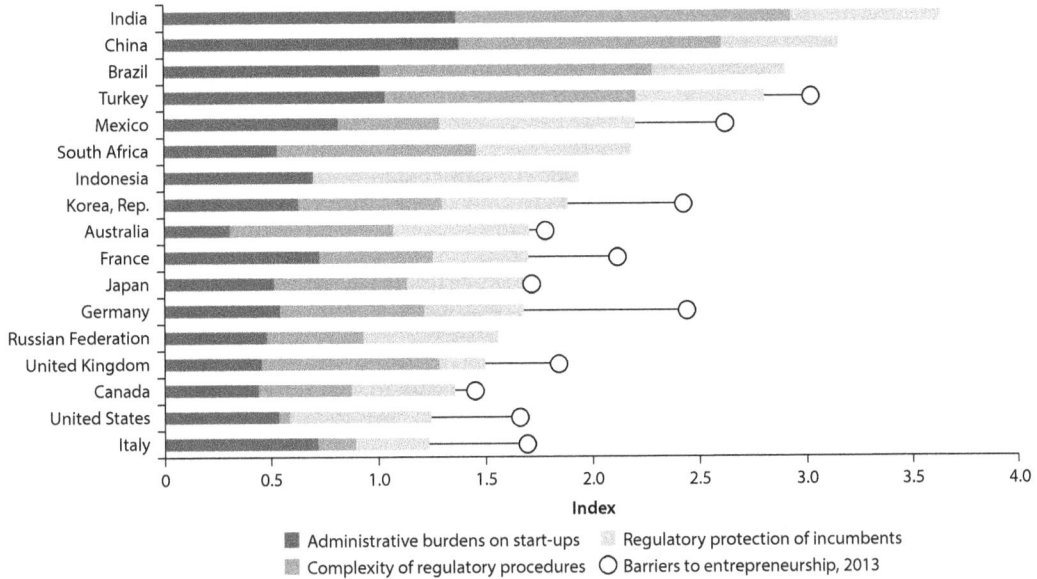

Legend:
- ■ Administrative burdens on start-ups
- ▨ Regulatory protection of incumbents
- ▨ Complexity of regulatory procedures
- ○ Barriers to entrepreneurship, 2013

Source: OECD, Product Market Regulation Database, www.oecd.org/economy/pmr, June 2015.
Note: The scale is 0–6, from least to most restrictive.

Figure 3.20 Average Size of Start-Ups and Old Firms across Industries and Countries

a. Manufacturing

b. Services

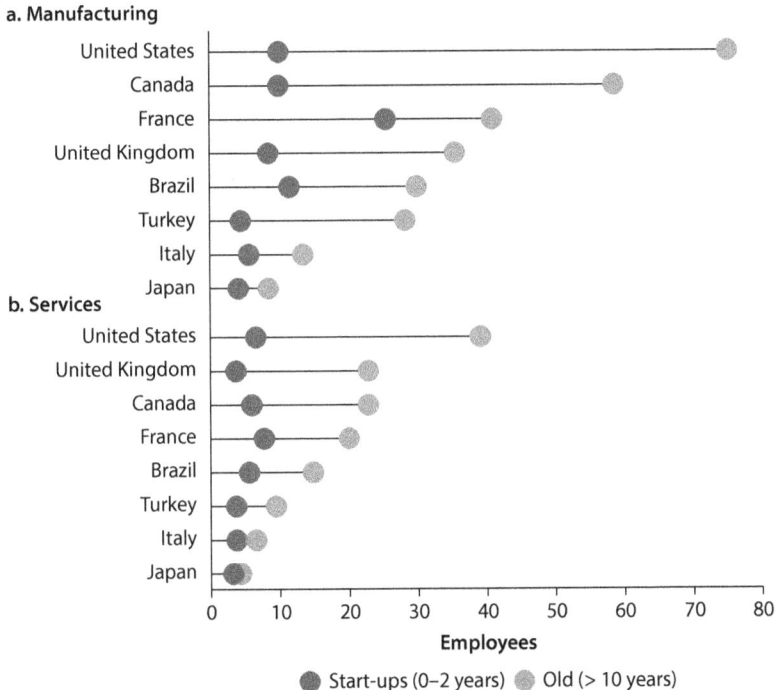

Legend:
- ● Start-ups (0–2 years)
- ● Old (> 10 years)

Sources: Criscuolo, Gal, and Menon 2014 and country submissions.

incumbents and other policy measures that delay the exit of less productive firms can stifle competition and slow the reallocation of resources from less to more productive firms. Examples include regulations that are less stringent for incumbents relative to entrants (for example, the so-called new source bias in environmental and health safety regulations), and support measures that are more generous for more established firms (for example, R&D tax credits that do not have carry-forward provisions). Perhaps most important, bankruptcy legislation that excessively penalizes failure is likely to reduce incentives for the efficient exit of less productive firms, which would otherwise free up resources for more productive uses. Enabling firms that are not successful to exit more easily might also contribute to stronger growth prospects for very productive and successful businesses.

Although entry and exit are clearly important, post-entry growth is even more critical for the potential scale that new SMEs can reach. Policies that (unwittingly) constrain the growth of young, innovative SMEs should be assessed with particular care. Examples include "sticks" (that is, regulations that affect only those firms above a certain size) and "carrots" (that is, support mechanisms for which only smaller firms are eligible). Further, policies that introduce distortions in factor (labor and capital) and product prices also affect post-entry growth, imposing constraints on the reallocation of resources toward more efficient firms. Those economic distortions, which reflect the presence of heterogeneous policy treatment of firms in the same industry, can impose significant barriers to firm growth. In this context, resources can be "trapped" in small and inefficient firms, serving as a drag on productivity growth and innovation at the firm and sector levels (Criscuolo, Gal, and Menon 2014).

Thus, focusing on the conditions that enable start-ups to grow to scale—if successful—or close down—if not successful—is important for a more dynamic, innovative, and global SME sector, as it can help generate more SMEs that are able to compete in international markets. An important difference is the extent to which some countries are more successful than others in channeling resources toward innovative and high-productivity SMEs that have the best opportunities to engage with foreign markets in GVCs.

Access to ICT Networks

Although engagement of SMEs in GVCs remains difficult, there are signs that some SMEs are managing to internationalize thanks to better access to ICT, including the Internet and mobile telecommunication. The Internet dramatically reduces the cost of finding buyers for SMEs, globally and domestically. Technology-enabled firms in low-income countries are much more likely to export, export to more destinations, and survive in the marketplace. Similarly, SMEs and new firms are likely to have a larger role in the export mix for technologically enabled trade than for traditional trade. Figure 3.21 shows comparisons between technologically enabled trade and digital trade for Jordan (eBay 2014); similar results are obtained for Chile, India, Indonesia, Peru, South Africa, Thailand, and Ukraine.

There is even some evidence on the emergence of so-called micro-multinationals, that is, small and young firms that are global from their inception. New ICT tools can facilitate cross-border e-commerce and participation in global markets for smaller and new entrants (for example, Skype for communications, Google and Dropbox for file sharing, LinkedIn for finding talent, PayPal for transactions, and eBay and Amazon for sales). Evidence shows that an increasing number of producers in low-income countries are selling using the Internet, either through their own websites or through web portals such as eBay and Alibaba. Business-to-consumer e-commerce[12] reached US$1.5 trillion globally in 2014 and is growing at 25 percent per year, and even more rapidly in the Asia-Pacific and Middle East and North Africa regions (table 3.1).[13] Business-to-business e-commerce may be even larger, and much of this trade is export trade. By 2020, global online sales will amount to US$10 trillion, with annual growth of 20 percent for business-to-consumer and 7.7 percent for business-to-business transactions. Much of that growth will originate in emerging markets, where the adoption of digital technology continues to rise rapidly.

Figure 3.21 Jordan: Performance of Technology-Enabled versus Traditional Exporters

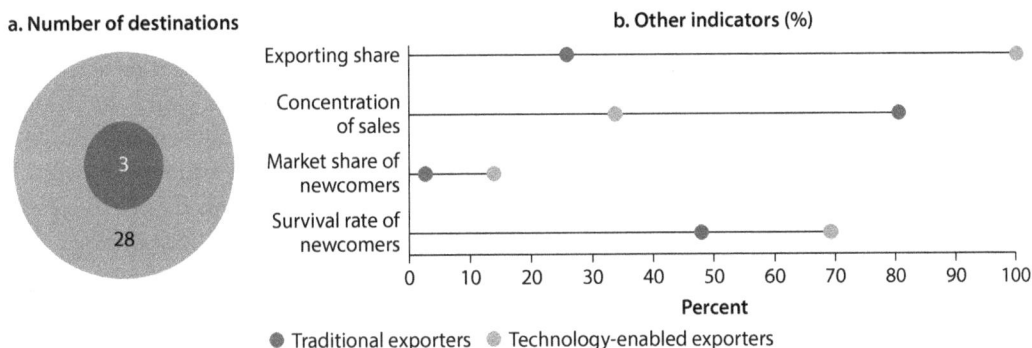

a. Number of destinations

b. Other indicators (%)

● Traditional exporters   ◉ Technology-enabled exporters

Source: eBay 2014, 33.

Table 3.1 Global Business-to-Consumer E-Commerce Marketplace, by Region, 2012–17
(US$, billions; average annual growth, %)

Region	2012	2013	2014	2015	2016	2017	CAGR (%)
Asia-Pacific	301.2	383.9	525.2	681.2	855.7	1052.9	50
North America	379.5	461.0	482.6	538.3	597.9	660.4	15
Western Europe	277.5	312.0	347.4	382.7	414.2	445.0	12
Central and Eastern Europe	41.5	49.5	58.0	64.4	68.9	73.1	15
Latin America	37.6	48.1	57.7	64.9	70.6	74.6	20
Middle East and Africa	20.6	27.0	33.8	69.5	45.5	51.4	30
Worldwide	1,058	1,215	1,505	1,771	2,053	2,357	25

Source: eMarketer, cited in Gordon and Suominen 2014.
Note: CAGR = compound annual growth rate.

Enhancing access to ICT networks and enabling SMEs to engage in e-commerce can be an effective way for small firms to go global and even grow across borders where they can become competitors in niche markets. Some are already taking advantage of those approaches. For example, M-Pesa, a Kenyan mobile money service, is now active across Africa, but also in Eastern Europe and South Asia. This way, it is connecting Kenyan jewelry artisans and fashion designers to customers around the world through mobile phones and an online marketplace. In Nepal, Young Innovations develops mobile apps, software solutions, and data analysis tools, thus engaging in the services trade.[14] In Serbia, the Farmia online marketplace leverages the Internet to bring farmers and buyers of livestock closer together, in an innovative, matchmaking information exchange and transport solution.[15] Innovations such as these, along with the many SME exporters using global platforms like eBay, Amazon, and Alibaba, are able to enhance their global reach substantially and reduce the transaction costs of trade.

Thus, enhancing the access of small firms to broadband networks can enable them to reach foreign markets more easily. The data and statistics available for OECD countries reveal a few important facts. In France and Korea, almost all small and medium-size firms now have such access (figure 3.22), but access is still below 90 percent in Turkey (for small firms, 10–49 employees) and Japan. It is the use that different firms make of such networks that matters, that is, firms are using the networks to engage in value chains or to outsource certain activities. In Italy, almost 40 percent of firms with 10–49 employees used cloud computing services in 2014, compared with 10 percent or fewer in France, Germany, and Korea. In Germany, almost 20 percent of firms with 10–49 employees in 2014 used supply chain management tools that automatically linked their business process to those of their suppliers, customers, or both. In Italy, that number was almost 14 percent, but only around 10 percent of small firms in France and the United Kingdom used such tools.

Figure 3.22 Broadband Connectivity, by Size of Firm, 2010 and 2013

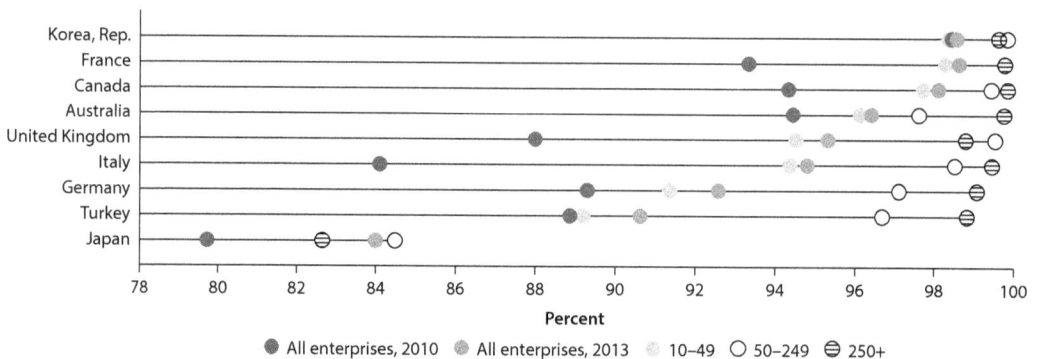

Source: OECD 2014.
Note: The relevant data for each firm size is for 2013.

Access to ICT networks is key to enable small firms to engage in electronic commerce, a low-cost way for firms to engage in trade, either to buy or sell. In Australia, almost 40 percent of small firms (with 10–49 employees) are engaged in electronic commerce, compared with less than 10 percent of such firms in Italy and Turkey (figure 3.23). Such engagement can contribute substantially to turnover; for example, in Korea, firms with 10–49 employees derived more than 28 percent of their turnover from electronic commerce in 2012, compared with only just over 2 percent in Italy.

Increasingly, electronic commerce crosses borders, sometimes going beyond the closest neighbors. For example, of all firms in Italy engaged in electronic commerce, 56 percent had sold to other European Union countries, and 38 percent to countries outside the European Union. In the United Kingdom, 34 percent of all firms engaged in electronic commerce had sold to countries outside the European Union, and some 24 percent of such firms in France and Germany (OECD 2014). Such commerce goes beyond business-to-business transactions and also involves consumers. For example, over 60 percent of Canadian consumers had ordered goods or services over the Internet from partner countries in 2013, mostly from the United States, although 20 percent had also bought from the rest of the world. In Turkey, only 4 percent of consumers had bought from partner countries, and only 2 percent from the rest of the world (OECD 2014).

The high cost of ICT adoption and lack of adequate financing help explain why smaller firms are less likely to adopt the technologies (OECD 2013a). Recent research points to a set of additional challenges: (a) reluctance of managers to adopt technological change, possibly because of a lack of knowledge, time, or mistrust; (b) consideration of the Internet's potential for cutting cost rather than expanding commercial opportunities; (c) costs of ICT infrastructure; (d) lack of ICT skills and expertise; and (e) lack of motivation or resources to train employees or recruit specialists (Consoli 2012).

Figure 3.23 Enterprises Engaged in Sales via E-Commerce by Employment Size, 2008 and 2012

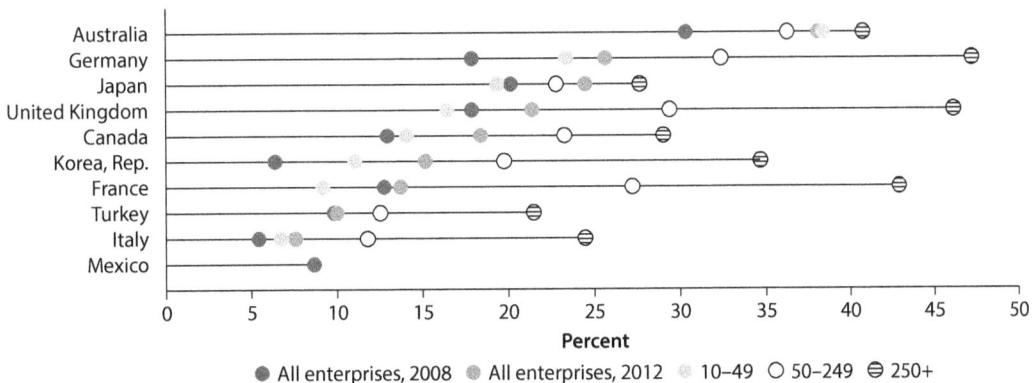

Source: OECD 2014.
Note: The relevant data for each firm size is for 2013.

The Internet—and ICT more generally—lowers important barriers for SMEs and entrepreneurship, but many potential gains could be lost without changes in the basic framework conditions facing SMEs. One important component concerns the regulatory burden. The administrative burden generated by governments for starting and running companies can be significant, but online government portals for information on business creation and registration can help lower the burden. There are also still barriers that limit competition that need to be addressed for economies to benefit fully from the Internet. Regulatory and trade barriers persistently inhibit entrepreneurs from accessing domestic and foreign markets.

For firms in low-income countries, further challenges exist, as there are significant impediments to the ability of SMEs to exploit the Internet fully for exporting. Over 60 percent of the world's population is still offline, inhibited by shortcomings in infrastructure, lack of basic and digital literacy, low incomes and high costs of going online, and weak incentives (McKinsey & Co. 2013). Infrastructure issues include access to electricity and building the Internet backbone—submarine cables and satellites, Internet exchange points, and "last-mile infrastructure" (OECD 2015b; Schumann and Kende 2013). In middle-income countries, many SMEs have Internet access but do not have websites through which they can do business, or they have limited understanding or capability of how to leverage the Internet as part of their business plan. For example, mobile application developers in Nepal struggle to launch their products in global app stores.

According to studies from the Arab Republic of Egypt, Argentina, China, India, South Africa, and Sri Lanka, entrepreneurs also face systemic and cultural barriers to digital trade—an important enabler of GVC participation, particularly in the services sector. These barriers include, among others, (a) inadequate or costly telecom infrastructure, including Internet access; (b) lack of digital literacy and skills, resulting in an unqualified labor force and uninformed consumers; (c) unclear legal and regulatory systems and standards; (d) difficulties with accessing electronic payment systems; (e) complex and unreliable logistics and distribution networks; and (f) lack of "one-stop-shop" facilities to ease digital trade. With regard to cultural barriers, digital trade can be hampered by (a) lack of face-to-face bargaining or social interactions, (b) distrust of online businesses and concerns about privacy and fraud, (c) low use of e-commerce by competitors and supply chain partners, (d) unclear benefits from e-commerce, (e) language barriers, and (f) perception of e-commerce as a costly and impractical way to do business.

Reducing existing barriers to digital trade, and thus improving access to global markets, will take a holistic approach. Multilateral organizations are working with clients to improve regulatory clarity, invest in digital literacy and entrepreneurship skills, identify digital economy opportunities in export markets, improve payment systems, and integrate SMEs into value chains.

Box 3.7 summarizes the take-away messages from this chapter.

Box 3.7 Key Take-Away Messages from Chapter 3

- Informality is one of the top five constraints for small firms in low-income countries in doing business, and a binding constraint to integrating into global value chains (GVCs).
- In the formal economy, the key challenge for suppliers integrating into or upgrading participation in GVCs is to increase productivity and access the necessary knowledge and technology to compete in international markets and upgrade to higher value-added activities. Broadening the skill set, innovating, and accessing foreign technology allow GVC suppliers to increase productivity and upgrade processes, products, and functions, and enter new, higher value-added sectors.
- Key *factors internal to the firm* that facilitate participation in GVCs include the following:
  - *Managerial and workforce skills.* Firms in low-income countries and some small and medium enterprises (SMEs) are plagued by weak managerial and workforce skills and inefficient organization. Those weaknesses are reflected in low levels of productivity, suboptimal use of the workforce, and waste of materials and inputs, which prevent the firm from supplying intermediate inputs at internationally competitive prices.
  - *Technology adoption.* Firms have much to gain by adopting new technologies. Technology adoption and knowledge absorption are particularly important priorities, as it is less costly and risky to acquire and use existing knowledge than to create new processes or products. Yet, for firms at the low end of the value chain, production scales that are too small and profit margins that are too narrow lengthen the recovery period of any fixed costs of investment and/or information acquisition.
  - *Innovation.* Innovation is an important requirement for the successful participation of SMEs in GVCs (OECD 2008). Process and organizational innovation increases firm productivity by reducing production costs, product innovation generates new and upgraded products, and marketing innovation differentiates firms' products from those of competitors, helping to increase market share.
- Internal capabilities alone are not sufficient. The ability of SMEs and firms in low-income countries to adopt new technologies swiftly, learn by doing, innovate, and optimize their production depends heavily on the operating environment, since the latter determines the costs of producing, exporting, and importing.
- External factors that matter are wide ranging. For suppliers from low-income countries, access to trade finance, transportation and shipping costs, inadequate infrastructure, and regulatory uncertainty (often tied to a complex business environment) are major obstacles according to surveys. Access to information about export opportunities and procedures and access to finance have emerged as the areas in which SMEs would value improvement most.
  - *Trade policy.* Trade policy remains a strategic policy area for ensuring success in GVCs. GVCs magnify the costs of protectionist measures, and trade costs fall disproportionately on SMEs and firms in low-income countries, given their often lower revenue base and structural market features. Good and cheap access to imports matters as much as access to foreign markets. Tariffs on inputs are particularly costly, because they are used directly in production and drive up costs. Market access in the international marketplace is restricted for several services that act as essential enablers in the geographic dispersion

box continues next page

Box 3.7 Key Take-Away Messages from Chapter 3 *(continued)*

of GVCs. Such services include information and communication technology (ICT), supply chain management services (to reduce inventories, shorten lead times, and enable faster customer response), and improved logistics services.

– *Trade infrastructure, connectivity, and trade facilitation measures.* Geography, good connectivity, and streamlined procedures for imports and exports are important determinants of countries' ability to join and strengthen participation in GVCs, and key factors in determining the costs of sourcing from and supplying to global markets. Getting to the border is one of the most pervasive constraints for exports of firms in low-income countries, and the costs of logistics services are disproportionately high for SMEs. Improving logistics is also where low-income countries have the most potential to reduce trade costs, according to recent survey information. And well-functioning trade facilitation measures enable GVC trade by reducing the time, cost, and uncertainty involved in importing and exporting.

– *Access to ICT networks.* Better access to ICT, including the Internet and mobile telecommunication, is an effective way to internationalize, in particular for firms engaged in digital trade. The Internet dramatically reduces the cost of finding buyers, globally and domestically, and ICT services enable SMEs to outsource some costly activities, reducing their costs and barriers to trade. Technology-enabled SMEs and firms in low-income countries are much more likely to export, export to more destinations, and survive in the marketplace.

– *Business environment and conditions that enable SMEs to reach scale.* Excessive regulations can affect firm dynamics (such as entry, firm growth, and exit) and GVC participation, by inducing an inefficient allocation of resources across firms and lowering productivity. Administrative burdens (red tape) and product market regulations can serve as barriers to entry, limiting the entry of young, innovative SMEs and restricting competition in the market. Policies that affect firm exit matter too. Subsidies to incumbents and other policy measures that delay the exit of less productive firms can stifle competition and slow the reallocation of resources from less to more productive firms. Examples include regulations that are less stringent for incumbents or fiscal measures that favor well-established firms over newcomers.

– *Quality and product certification and international standards.* Certification of quality and products, and compliance with international standards are another relevant challenge for SMEs and firms in low-income countries to participate in GVCs. Competitive pressures in global markets require firms to produce at world-class standards of quality, and consumers are increasingly attentive to production conditions. Low labor and production costs are increasingly insufficient as a motivation for lead firms to invest in and source from low-income countries.

– *Access to finance.* Access to external sources of funding is critical to finance SMEs, and trade finance is one of the top perceived constraints by firms in low-income countries. Size and the intangibility of assets play against the creditworthiness ratings of many SMEs. Trade finance is also likely to be a constraint to engaging in enhancing productivity, as informational asymmetries (for example, adverse selection and moral hazard problems) create a gap between the private innovation rate of return and the cost of capital when the innovation investor and financier are different entities. Access to risk capital is an additional constraint for innovative SMEs that are seeking to grow and achieve a sufficient scale.

Notes

1. As Paul Krugman (1994, 11) famously claimed, "Productivity isn't everything, but in the long run it is almost everything. A country's ability to improve its standard of living over time depends almost entirely on its ability to raise its output per worker."

2. This idea is partly spurred by the oft-cited iPad case study, which highlights the low share of value added that assembly occupies in the production process—less than 5 percent of the sale value of the iPad remains in China. This example has been used to justify policy objectives that seek to increase the *share* of the firm's value added in a given product.

3. The authors would like to thank Matthew Gamser, Chief Operations Officer from the World Bank Group, for the inputs he provided.

4. Data in this section are taken from two reports from the World Bank Group. G20 analysis is from a report for the Global Partnership for Financial Inclusion and the Investment and Infrastructure Working Group, April 23, 2015. The findings for the European Union are from a World Bank presentation to the European Commission on its Green Paper on Capital Markets Integration, January 30, 2015.

5. World Bank Survey, March 2015, Basel II: Proposed Revisions to the Standardised Approach to Credit Risk. See also GPFI/SME Finance Forum, Small and Medium Enterprise Finance: New Findings, Trends and G20/Global Partnership for Financial Inclusion Progress, Washington, DC, August 2013.

6. The idea that innovation is difficult to finance in a freely competitive marketplace dates back to the articles by Nelson (1959) and Arrow (1962). In particular, two characteristics of the innovation process make innovation finance more difficult: (a) innovation produces an intangible asset, and (b) the returns to innovation investment are highly uncertain. See Hall and Lerner (2009) and Kerr and Nanda (2014) for a review. Intangible assets do not typically constitute accepted collateral to obtain external funding. Much of the knowledge created in innovation processes is tacit rather than codified and embedded in the human capital of a firm's employees (who can leave) and its organizational capital. Even when this knowledge is codified and registered—for instance, in the form of a patent—its value is difficult to measure. Further, the distribution of returns is highly skewed. There is a large probability of failure and a small probability of huge success. Since quantifying the probability of success and failure is typically impossible, the expected return to that investment cannot be estimated. This uncertainty creates significant problems for the standard risk adjustment methods used by funding providers. Two types of uncertainty are typically present—technological uncertainty and market uncertainty—and the mixture of them can vary substantially (Bravo-Biosca, Cusolito, and Hill 2015).

7. World Bank Trade Cost Dataset web page, http://data.worldbank.org/data-catalog/trade-costs-dataset.

8. The study found that in 2004 the effective tariff rate was 17 percent higher than the nominal rate in the United States, 46 percent higher in Korea, and as much as 116 and 171 percent higher in China and Mexico, respectively, because of multiple border crossings in trade.

9. These effects may appear large, but it should be noted that the tariff reductions in the example are sizable, around 10 percentage points.

10. See the OECD Services Trade Restrictiveness Index, http://www.oecd.org/trade/services-trade-restrictiveness-index.htm.

11. http://www.apec.org/About-Us/About-APEC/Business-Resources/APEC-Business
-Travel-Card.aspx, http://www.apec.org/about-us/about-apec/business-resources
/apec-business-travel-card.aspx

12. The terms *e-commerce, e-trade*, and *digital trade* are used interchangeably in this report.

13. See eMarketer, cited in Gordon and Suominen (2014).

14. Young Innovations website, http://younginnovations.com.np/.

15. Farmia website, http://farmia.co/.

References

Acs, Zoltan J., and David B. Audretsch. 1987. "Innovation, Market Structure and Firm Size." *Review of Economics and Statistics* 69 (4): 567–75.

Allen, Richard, and Duncan Last. 2007. "Low-Income Countries Need Upgrades." *IMF Survey Magazine*, July 19.

Andrews, Dan, and Federico Cingano. 2014. "Public Policy and Resource Allocation: Evidence from Firms in OECD Countries." *Economic Policy* 29 (78): 253–96.

Andrews, Dan, and Chiara Criscuolo. 2013. "Knowledge-Based Capital, Innovation and Resource Allocation." OECD Economics Department Working Paper 1046, OECD Publishing, Paris.

APEC Policy Support Unit 2011. "Reducing Business Travel Costs: The Success of APEC's Business Mobility Initiatives."

Arrow, Kenneth. 1962. "Economic Welfare and the Allocation of Resources for Inventions." In *The Rate and Direction of Inventive Activity: Economic and Social Factors*, edited by R. R. Nelson. Princeton, NJ: Princeton University Press.

Arvis, Jean-Francois, Gaël Raballand, and Jean-François Marteau. 2010. "The Cost of Being Landlocked: Logistics Costs and Supply Chain Reliability." World Bank, Washington, DC.

Arvis, Jean-François, Yann Duval, Ben Shepherd, and Chorthip Utoktham. 2013. "Trade Costs in the Developing World, 1995–2010." Policy Research Working Paper 6309, World Bank, Washington, DC.

Arvis, Jean-François, Ben Shepherd, Yann Duval, and Chorthip Utoktham. 2013. "Trade Costs and Development: A New Data Set." Economic Premise Note 104, World Bank, Washington, DC.

Baldwin, Richard. 2006. "Managing the Noodle Bowl: The Fragility of East Asian Regionalism." CEPR DP 5561; published in *Singapore Economic Review* 53 (3): 449–78, 2008.

Bitran, E., S. Nieto-Parra, and J. S. Robledo. 2013. "Opening the Black Box of Contract Renegotiations: An Analysis of Road Concessions in Chile, Colombia and Peru." OECD Development Centre Working Paper 317, OECD Publishing, Paris.

Blomström, Magnus, and Ari Kokko. 1998. "Multinational Corporations and Spillovers." *Journal of Economic Surveys* 12 (3): 247–77.

Bloom, Nicholas, Benn Eiffert, Aprajit Mahajan, David McKenzie, and John Roberts. 2012. "Does Management Really Matter? Evidence from India." *Quarterly Journal of Economics* (2013) 128 (1): 1–51.

Bloom, Nicholas B., Raffaella Sadun, and John Van Reenen. 2013. "Management as a Technology?" Research paper, Stanford University, Stanford, CA.

Bravo-Biosca, A., A. Cusolito, and J. Hill. 2015. "Financing Business Innovation. A Review of External Sources of Funding for Innovative Businesses and Public Policies to Support Them." World Bank, Washington, DC.

Cadot, Olivier, and Mariem Malouche. 2012. "Overview." In *Non-Tariff Measures: A Fresh Look at Trade Policy's New Frontier*, edited by Olivier Cadot and Mariem Malouche, 1–19. Washington, DC: World Bank.

Consoli, D. 2012. "Literature Analysis on Determinant Factors and the Impact of ICT in SMEs." *Procedia–Social and Behavioral Sciences* 62: 93–97. http://dx.doi.org/10.1016/j.sbspro.2012.09.016.

Criscuolo, C., P. Gal, and C. Menon. 2014. "The Dynamics of Employment Growth: New Evidence from 18 Countries." OECD Science, Technology and Industry Policy Paper 14, OECD Publishing, Paris. http://dx.doi.org/10.1787/5jz417hj6hg6-en.

de Rassenfosse, Gaétan, and Annelies Wastin. 2011. "Selection Bias in Innovation Studies: A Simple Test." Centre for European Economic Research Discussion Paper 12-012. SSRN:http://ssrn.com/abstract=2014681orhttp://dx.doi.org/10.2139/ssrn.2014681.

Disdier, Anne-Celia, Lionel Fontagne, and Mondher Mimouni. 2008. "The Impact of Regulations on Agricultural Trade: Evidence from the SPS and TBT Agreements." *American Journal of Agricultural Economics* 90 (2): 336–50.

eBay Inc. 2014. *Commerce 3.0 for Development: The Promise of the Global Empowerment Network*. An eBay Report based on an Empirical Study Conducted by Sidley Austin LLP. San Jose, CA: eBay.

Estevadeordal, Antoni, and Alan M. Taylor. 2009. "Is the Washington Consensus Dead? Growth, Openness, and the Great Liberation." IDB Working Paper 138, Inter-American Development Bank, Washington, DC.

Ewens, Michael, and Christian Fons-Rosen. 2013. "The Consequences of Entrepreneurial Firm Founding on Innovation." Social Science Research Network, Rochester, NY. http://ssrn.com/abstract=2291811 or http://dx.doi.org/10.2139/ssrn.2291811.

Fair Labor Association. 2012. *Foxconn Verification Status Report*. Washington, DC: Fair Labor Association.

Farole, Thomas, and Deborah Winkler. 2014. *Making Foreign Direct Investment Work for Sub-Saharan Africa*. Washington, DC: World Bank.

Freund, Caroline, and Nadia Rocha. 2010. "What Constrains Africa's Exports?" Policy Research Working Paper 5184, World Bank, Washington, DC.

Gereffi, Gary, and Karina Fernandez-Stark. 2010. "The Offshore Services Value Chain, Developing Countries and the Crisis." Policy Research Working Paper 5262, World Bank, Washington, DC.

Gordon, Reena B., and Kati Suominen. 2014. "Going Global: Promoting the Internationalization of Small and Mid-Size Enterprises in Latin America and the Caribbean." Inter-American Development Bank, Washington, DC.

Hall, Bronwyn H., and Josh Lerner. 2009. "The Financing of R&D and Innovation." NBER Working Paper 15325, National Bureau of Economic Research, Cambridge, MA.

Hiratsuka, D. 2005. "Vertical Intra-Regional Production Networks in East Asia: A Case Study of the Hard Disk Drive Industry." In *East Asia's De Facto Economic Integration*, edited by D. Hiratsuka. London: Palgrave McMillan.

Hummels, David, Volodymyr Lugovskyy, and Alexandre Skiba. 2007. "The Trade Reducing Effects of Market Power in International Shipping." NBER Working Paper 12914, National Bureau of Economic Research, Cambridge, MA.

Iacovone, Leonardo, and Qursum Qasim. 2013. "Entrepreneurship Policy Brief: A Tool for Analysis and Promotion." World Bank, Washington, DC.

Jaffee, Steve. 2006. "Sanitary and Phytosanitary Regulation: Overcoming Constraints." In *Trade, Doha, and Development: A Window into the Issues*, edited by Richard Newfarmer, 353–70. Washington, DC: World Bank.

Javorcik, Beata Smarzynska. 2004. "Does Foreign Direct Investment Increase the Productivity of Domestic Firms? In Search of Spillovers through Backward Linkages." *American Economic Review* 94 (3): 605–27.

Jensen, Michael F., and John C. Keyser. 2012. "Standards Harmonisation and Trade: The Case of the East African Dairy Industry." In *Non-Tariff Measures: A Fresh Look at Trade Policy's New Frontier*, edited by Olivier Cadot and Mariem Malouche, 187–209. Washington, DC: World Bank.

Johansson, Åsa, and Eduardo Olaberría. 2014. "Global Trade and Specialisation Patterns over the Next 50 Years." OECD Economic Policy Paper 10, OECD Publishing, Paris.

Kerr, William R., and Ramana Nanda. 2014. "Financing Innovation." NBER Working Paper 20676, National Bureau of Economic Research, Cambridge, MA.

Koopman, Robert, William Powers, Zhi Wang, and Wei Shang-Jin. 2010. "Give Credit Where Credit Is Due: Tracing Value Added in Global Production." NBER Working Paper 16426, National Bureau of Economic Research, Cambridge, MA.

Kowalski, Przemyslaw, Javier Lopez Gonzalez, Alexandros Ragoussis, and Cristian Ugarte. 2015. "Participation of Developing Countries in Global Value Chains: Implications for Trade and Trade-Related Policies." OECD Trade Policy Paper 179, OECD Publishing, Paris.

Krugman, Paul. 1994. *The Age of Diminished Expectations*. Cambridge, MA: MIT Press.

Limão, Nuno, and Anthony J. Venables. 2001. "Infrastructure, Geographical Disadvantage, Transport Costs, and Trade." *World Bank Economic Review* 15 (3): 451–79.

Mason, Colin, and Jennifer Kwok. 2010. "Investment Readiness Programmes and Access to Finance: A Critical Review of Design Issues." *Local Economy* 25 (4): 269–92.

Mayer, Frederick, and Gary Gereffi. 2010. "Regulation and Economic Globalization: Prospects and Limits of Private Governance." *Business and Politics* 12 (3).

Mayer, Frederick W., and John Pickles. 2010. "Re-Embedding Governance: Global Apparel Value Chains and Decent Work." Capturing the Gains Working Paper 2010/1, Department for International Development, Manchester, UK.

McKinsey & Company. 2013. "Offline and Falling Behind: Barriers to Internet Adoption." McKinsey & Company, San Francisco, CA.

McLinden, Gerard. 2013. "Single-Window Systems: What We Have Learned." *Trade Post* (blog), World Bank, April 30. http://blogs.worldbank.org/trade/single-window -systems-what-we-have-learned.

Ministry of Economy, Trade, and Industry (Japan). 2012. "The Survey on Global Value Chain." Ministry of Economy, Trade, and Industry, Tokyo.

Mitsubishi UFJ Research & Consulting. 2012. "Survey of Business Startup Conditions." Commissioned by the Small and Medium Enterprise Agency, Tokyo.

Nelson, Andrew. 2008. "Travel Time to Major Cities: A Global Map of Accessibility." Office for Official Publications of the European Communities, Luxembourg. doi:10.2788/95835.

Nelson, Richard R. 1959. "The Economics of Invention: A Survey of the Literature." *Journal of Business* 32: 101.

Nielsen, Peter Bøegh, ed. 2008. *International Sourcing—Moving Business Functions Abroad.* Copenhagen: Statistics Denmark. http://www.dst.dk/publ/InterSourcing.

Nordås, Hildegunn Kyvik, and Roberta Piermartini. 2004. "Infrastructure and Trade." WTO Staff Working Paper ERSD-2004-04, Economic Research and Statistics Division, World Trade Organization, Geneva.

OECD (Organisation for Economic Co-operation and Development). 2008. *Enhancing the Role of SMEs in Global Value Chains.* Paris: OECD Publishing.

———. 2011a. "The Impact of Trade Liberalisation on Jobs and Growth: Technical Note." OECD Trade Policy Working Paper 107, OECD Publishing, Paris.

———. 2011b. *Intellectual Assets and Innovation: The SME Dimension.* Paris: OECD Publishing.

———. 2012. "A Survey of Policy Makers." Prepared for the OECD project on Fostering Small and Medium-Sized Participation in the Global Market, OECD Centre for SMEs, Entrepreneurship, and Local Development, Paris.

———. 2013a. *Interconnected Economies: Benefiting from Global Value Chains.* OECD Synthesis Report, OECD, Paris. doi:10.1787/9789264189560-en.

———. 2013b. *Perspectives on Global Development 2013: Industrial Policies in a Changing World.* OECD Publishing, Paris. doi:10.1787/persp_glob_dev-2013-en.

———. 2013c. "Trade Policy Implications of Global Value Chains: Case Studies." OECD Trade Policy Paper 161, OECD Publishing, Paris. doi:10.1787/5k3tpt2t0zs1-en.

———. 2014. *Measuring the Digital Economy: A New Perspective.* Paris: OECD Publishing.

———. 2015a. *OECD Innovation Strategy 2015: An Agenda for Policy Action.* Paris: OECD Publishing.

———. 2015b. *Digital Economy Outlook 2015.* Paris: OECD Publishing.

———. 2015c. *Science, Technology and Industry Scoreboard 2015.* Paris: OECD Publishing.

———. 2015d. *The Future of Productivity.* Paris: OECD.

OECD and WTO (Organisation for Economic Co-operation and Development and World Trade Organization). 2013. *Aid for Trade at a Glance 2011: Showing Results Emerging from the Case Stories.* Paris and Geneva: OECD and WTO.

OECD, WTO, and UNCTAD (Organisation for Economic Co-operation and Development, World Trade Organization, and United Nations Conference on Trade and Development). 2013. *Implications of Global Value Chains for Trade, Investment, Development, and Jobs.* Report prepared for the G20 Leaders Summit, St. Petersburg, Russian Federation, September 5–6. http://www.oecd.org/sti/ind/G20-Global-Value-Chains-2013.pdf.

OECD, WTO, and World Bank (Organisation for Economic Co-operation and Development, World Trade Organization, and World Bank). 2014. *Global Value Chains: Challenges, Opportunities, and Implications for Policy.* Report prepared for the G20 Trade Ministers Meeting, Sydney, July 19.

Raballand, Gaël, Salim Refas, Monica Beuran, and Gözde Isik. 2012. *Why Does Cargo Spend Weeks in Sub-Saharan African Ports? Lessons from Six Countries.* Washington, DC: World Bank.

Rodríguez-Clare, Andrés. 1996. "Multinationals, Linkages, and Economic Development." *American Economic Review* 86 (4): 852–73.

Sangho, Yéyandé, Patrick Labaste, and Christophe Ravry. 2010. "Growing Mali's Mango Exports: Linking Farmers to Markets through Innovations in the Value Chain." World Bank, Washington, DC.

Schumann, Robert, and Michael Kende. 2013. *Lifting Barriers to Internet Development in Africa: Suggestions for Improving Connectivity*. London: Analysys Mason Limited.

SIMES. 2012. "The Mediterranean Partnership Fund." SIMES, Rome.

Stone, Susan, James Messent, and Dorothee Flaig. 2016. "Emerging Policy Issues: Localisation Barriers to Trade." OECD Trade Policy Paper 180, OECD Publishing, Paris.

Straube, Frank, Robert Handfield, Hans-Christian Pfohl, and Andreas Wieland. 2013. *Trends und Strategien in Logistik und Supply Chain Management*. Hamburg, Germany: Deutscher Verkehrs-Verlag.

Sturgeon, Timothy, Gary Gereffi, Andrew Guinn, and Ezequiel Zylberberg. 2013. *A Indústria Brasileira e as Cadeias Globais de Valor: Uma Análise Com Base nas Indústrias Aeronáutica, de Dispositivos Médicos e de Eletrônicos*. Rio de Janeiro: Elsevier.

Taglioni, Daria, and Deborah Winkler. 2016. "Making Value Chains Work for Development." World Bank, Washington, DC.

USITC (United States International Trade Commission). 2013a. *The Economic Effects of Significant US Import Restraints: Eighth Update 2013. Special Topic: Services' Contribution to Manufacturing*. USITC Publication 4440, Washington, DC.

———. 2013b. *Global Value Chains: Investment and Trade for Development*. World Investment Report, UNCTAD, Geneva.

van Tongeren, Frank, John Beghin, and Stéphane Marette. 2009. "A Cost-Benefit Framework for the Assessment of Non-Tariff Measures in Agro-Food Trade." OECD Food, Agriculture, and Fisheries Working Paper 21, OECD Publishing, Paris.

van Tongeren, Frank, Anne-Célia Disdier, Joanna Ilicic-Komorowska, Stéphane Marette, and Martin von Lampe. 2010. "Case Studies of Costs and Benefits of Non-Tariff Measures: Cheese, Shrimp, and Flowers." OECD Food, Agriculture, and Fisheries Working Paper 28, OECD Publishing, Paris.

Wang, Jian-Ye, and Magnus Blomström. 1992. "Foreign Investment and Technology Transfer: A Simple Model." *European Economic Review* 36 (1): 137–55.

Wilson, K. 2015. "Policy Lessons from Financing Innovative Firms." OECD Science, Technology and Industry Policy Paper 24, OECD Publishing, Paris.

CHAPTER 4

Policies to Promote the Participation of SMEs and Low-Income Countries in GVCs

Introduction

There are opportunities for small and medium enterprises (SMEs) and firms in low-income countries to integrate into global value chains (GVCs); increase productivity and upgrade products, processes, and functions within GVCs; and transition to more productive activities and sectors. These opportunities depend not only on the types of GVCs in which they operate, but also on external and internal factors that affect firms throughout their life cycle.

As emphasized in previous analyses submitted to the Group of Twenty (G20) (see, in particular, OECD, WTO, and UNCTAD 2013; OECD, WTO, and World Bank 2014), openness to trade and investment, efficient services regulations, and open access to information flows through, inter alia, efficient telecommunications services are preconditions for success in international markets; however, alone they are insufficient. External constraints may also originate from an unfriendly business environment and the firm's (lack of) access to capital, labor, technology, and other inputs.

Internal constraints also matter, including the capabilities of the entrepreneur to innovate and adopt new technologies, the management and organization of the firm, and the capacity of the firm to tap into relevant networks. In short, for the wider private sector to thrive from countries' participation in GVCs, appropriate policy frameworks are needed that allow countries and firms to capitalize on their existing productive capacities and create spillover benefits from foreign investment, knowledge, and innovations. This chapter builds on the previous two reports to the G20 and focuses in addition to elements of critical importance to SMEs and low-income countries.

Successful GVC participation by firms in low-income countries and SMEs in all countries requires that reforms are implemented as coherent packages. It also requires a sustained, coordinated, and long-term approach based on the design of incentive mechanisms that are tailored to the specific needs of countries, types of firms, and value chains. Two sets of concurrent actions are necessary: furthering openness and ensuring that the benefits trickle down (to SMEs) and across (to low-income countries), while also building the necessary supporting measures for maximizing dynamic gains.

Furthering International Trade Openness

Trade-related reforms have been at the center of the agenda of G20 trade ministers in recent years. But much still needs to be done, and—for many countries—that includes reordering priorities on trade policy. Facilitating imports and ensuring timeliness in the two-way flows of goods are as important as facilitating exports and market access. Improving trade-related infrastructure and streamlining border management are obvious priorities, but for many economies, improving the efficiency of the services sector, increasing competition in the domestic economy, and addressing nontariff measures that unnecessarily raise the price of imported inputs are equally important.

Trade Facilitation

Trade facilitation has become central to the economic agenda of every world region. Tackling some of the key barriers that saddle traders in low-income countries with high trade costs and long delays will result in increased bilateral trade, greater export diversification, enhanced foreign investment, and improved national competitiveness.

The Organisation for Economic Co-operation and Development (OECD) has developed a set of trade facilitation indicators that identify areas for action and enable the potential impact of reforms to be assessed. These indicators cover the full spectrum of border procedures, from advance rulings to transit guarantees, for more than 160 countries across income levels, geographical regions, and development stages. Analysis shows that trade facilitation measures can benefit all countries in their roles as exporters, as well as importers, allowing better access to inputs for production and greater participation in GVCs. Analysis of the indicators also shows that comprehensive trade facilitation reform is more effective than isolated or piecemeal measures (figure 4.1). The potential reduction in trade costs of all the trade facilitation measures adds up to almost 15 percent for low-income countries, 16 percent for lower-middle-income countries, 13 percent for upper-middle-income countries, and 10 percent for OECD countries.

The Trade Facilitation Agreement (TFA) reached in Bali in 2013 by the members of the World Trade Organization (WTO) is an important step toward facilitating trade. The TFA allows WTO members to customize implementation of the agreement according to their capacities and technical assistance needs, along with a better support structure to help target, monitor, and coordinate implementation. As of May 2016, 79 out of 162 members, including Cambodia,

Figure 4.1 Trade Facilitation Measures: Potential Cost Reduction in Goods Trade

a. Low-income countries

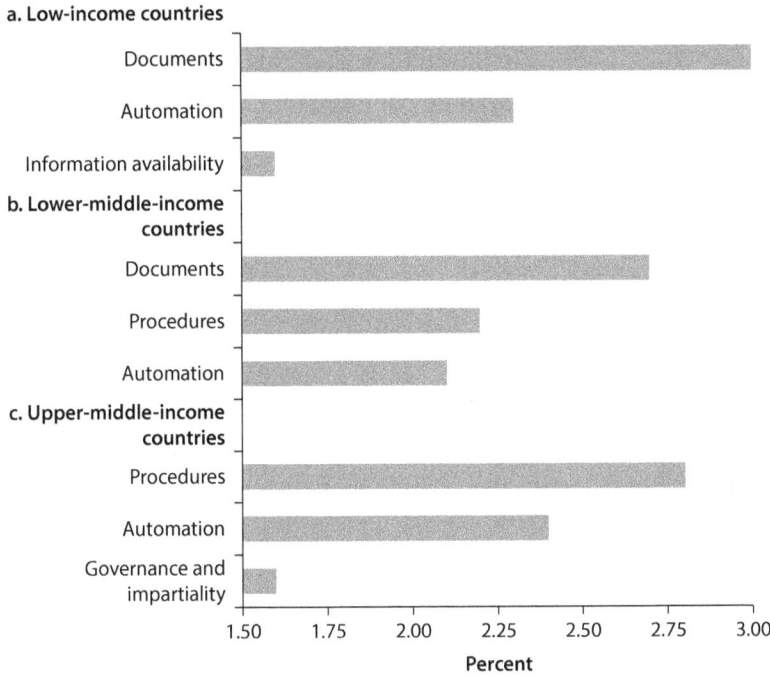

Source: OECD, WTO, and UNCTAD 2013.

China, the European Union, India, and the United States, have already ratified. The WTO TFA will come into force when two-thirds of WTO members have lodged their protocols of ratification.

Early implementation of the TFA is not only a sign that the implementation objective of the G20's 2015 agenda has been achieved, but also a "win-win" situation for all countries. The benefits fall disproportionality to low-income countries, as their traders typically face significantly higher costs that reduce their capacity to compete in regional and international markets (as demonstrated by the evidence in figure 4.1). For this reason, the World Bank Group has been a major supporter of trade facilitation for many years and has financed more than 120 projects and many technical assistance activities that are closely aligned with the measures included in the TFA. The World Bank Group's current trade and integration portfolio totals US$13.3 billion, with more than half devoted to trade facilitation. The results have been aimed at improvements in areas such as customs and border management, streamlined documentation requirements, trade infrastructure investment, port efficiency, transport security, logistics and transport services, regional trade facilitation and trade corridors, transit, and multimodal transport. This type of concrete, practical assistance is critical to improving the national competitiveness of the poorest countries in the world.

Although all measures covered by the TFA offer genuine benefits to the trading community, experience suggests that regionally integrated facilitation frameworks similar to that of the European Union are also necessary. Moreover, early efforts to strengthen stakeholder coordination through the establishment of national trade facilitation committees can have a very positive impact on building and sustaining momentum for reform. The OECD finds that in Indonesia and the Philippines, for example, reforms in border agency cooperation rendered clearance processes less opaque, enabling traders to plan more confidently, supporting just-in-time processes, and reducing the costs associated with uncertainty (OECD, WTO, and World Bank 2014). In general, stakeholder coordination has proved critical to supporting the implementation of complex, long-term projects, such as establishing trade information portals and single-window regimes. In line with this thinking, the World Bank Group is focusing increased attention on (a) the establishment of appropriate national governance and coordination mechanisms and (b) the design phase of projects to ensure appropriate sequencing of reforms.

The international community, multilateral organizations, and the G20 can do a lot to help low-income countries and their SMEs maximize the benefits from ongoing trade facilitation efforts. The international community can help by taking an active role in multilateral and regional negotiations, as well as by assisting low-income countries in effectively implementing all aspects of TFAs in ways that ensure genuine trade facilitation benefits for the trading community. It can help in the following ways:

• Implement trade facilitation reforms as coherent packages of hard and soft infrastructure. The international community can further foster strategies designed to assist countries in effectively implementing all aspects of multilateral and regional TFAs in ways that ensure genuine trade facilitation benefits for the trading community, rather than mere compliance with the legal text. Development institutions should respond as rapidly as possible to demand from low-income countries, with customized approaches to meet specific needs, operational circumstances, and national trade facilitation priorities, providing a continuum of potential trade facilitation support activities that are aligned with the principles of the agreements. Those include on-the-ground gap assessments to validate needs, project design assistance to support the development of practical implementation plans, and, where appropriate, identification of sources of financing for implementation projects, support for establishing and strengthening national trade facilitation committees, provision of short- to medium-term technical assistance and capacity-building support to implement specific measures and build implementation momentum, and support for regional solutions to support and facilitate regional integration.

• Facilitate information on costs, benefits, and implementation challenges, and provide practical guidelines on establishing technical support and capacity building for reform, which are important and concrete ways to help low-income countries and SMEs. That includes providing countries with practical guidelines on establishing a technical support mechanism for negotiators in agreements, including real-time analysis and advice on the content and cost implications of the proposals tabled (see, for example, the *Trade Facilitation Support Guide* developed by the World Bank Group). It also includes providing practical information to countries and their firms on the potential costs and implementation challenges of various agreements (see, for example, the in-country assessments by the World Bank Group, International Monetary Fund, and World Customs Organization).

- Enhance cooperation and coordination between development partners at the multilateral, regional, and bilateral levels to avoid duplications and to support regional activities of trade facilitation and programs integrating national and regional aspects. Ongoing efforts in these areas include the World Bank Group's support to regional bodies, including the West African Economic and Monetary Union (UEMOA), the Central African Economic and Monetary Community, the Common Market for Eastern and Southern Africa, and the Economic Community of West African States in Africa, as well as the Association of Southeast Asian Nations in East Asia. In the case of the UEMOA, support started with a TFA needs assessment of each of the eight member states. In turn, this new program will drive a series of technical assistance activities at the regional and national levels. Regional activities are particularly useful if they are directed toward improving the efficiency of gateway ports, streamlining and harmonizing land border-crossing procedures, revising legislation, and—given the importance of efficient transit arrangements for landlocked countries—improving the operation of transit regimes through regional integration and trade corridor projects.

- Identify practical means for harnessing private sector contributions to the implementation process of trade facilitation initiatives. This may include partnering with major industry associations to identify and support trade facilitation–related initiatives that provide a strong demonstration effect. It also means contributing to forums, such as the Global Facilitation Partnership for Trade and Transport, which bring together international and regional organizations as well as private sector associations and companies interested in facilitating trade.

- Conduct analytical work for monitoring and evaluating the performance and design of policy. The OECD heralds such work with a variety of tools. The World Bank Group prepares the Logistics Performance Index and the Doing Business survey, which provide focused analytical tools, indicators, and data sets to assist national policy makers and development partners in identifying and tackling key trade facilitation bottlenecks. These tools are used to guide efforts in the design and implementation of targeted trade facilitation projects.

Logistics Infrastructure and Services and Policies Affecting Their Use

Trade facilitation alone cannot lead to an effective and substantial strategy of participation in higher value-added trade and investment attraction, particularly by SMEs and firms in low-income countries. It can only be an element of a wider strategy. Infrastructure and ancillary services also need to be developed. Infrastructure needs to cover areas as diverse as the development of ports, roads, cargo-handling facilities, and broadband and other information and communication technology (ICT) systems. Experience shows the complementarities between hard and soft interventions, especially in low-income regions. For example, improvements in trade facilitation are implemented more easily with physical investment to develop or rehabilitate international transport infrastructure, such as road or rail corridors.

Logistics infrastructure and efficiency are now high on the agenda of policy makers, private firms, and international organizations. In this case, as in the case of trade facilitation, reforms must be implemented as coherent packages, and they require sustained, long-term attention. There is not one unique institutional arrangement for countries to implement logistics-related reforms. Policy making is a responsibility shared among the government agencies in charge of transportation policies and investment, commerce, industry, and customs and border management. No country has a ministry for logistics. Instead, a collective framework that includes the private sector is important for consistent implementation. Canada, China, Finland, Germany, Malaysia, and Morocco have all introduced councils or similar coordination mechanisms.

The focus and leadership of logistics reforms depend on local circumstances. In high-income and emerging economies, transportation agencies have often led the coordination, increasingly with an environmental focus. In low-income countries, the agencies in charge of commerce and economic development have also played a major role in promoting the facilitation and logistics agenda.

In this area as well, the international community, multilateral organizations, and the G20 can help with a combination of hard and soft interventions, including the following:

- Information on costs, benefits, and implementation challenges and practical guidelines on establishing technical support and capacity building for reform.
- Assistance to countries in effectively implementing all aspects of logistics and transport reform in ways that ensure genuine benefits for the trading community and SMEs. This implies customizing approaches to meet specific needs, operational circumstances, and national connectivity priorities, as well as providing a continuum of potential support activities, including (a) logistics performance assessments, (b) development of practical implementation plans, (c) identification of sources of financing for implementation plans, and (d) support for the chosen domestic institutional arrangement to implement logistics-related reforms.
- Cooperation and coordination between development partners, including multilateral institutions, regional development banks, donors, and other stakeholders to ensure effective coordination and to minimize the possibility of needless duplication.

- Identification of practical means for harnessing private sector contributions to the implementation process of reform initiatives in the logistics sector, including partnering with major industry associations and key players in logistics.
- Analytical work for monitoring and evaluating the performance and design of policy is also important and should continue to be developed.

Trade Policy

Trade policy matters. Along with domestic reform, it is a powerful engine of GVC integration, provided that it responds rapidly and effectively. "Trade policy as usual" needs some adjustments when thinking about GVCs and the participation of SMEs and low-income countries.

GVCs are the new lens that underscores the importance for policy makers to fully appreciate the importance of the synergies between the core areas of trade and investment regulation and well-tailored complementary measures. In most countries, many agencies have a role in setting and enforcing regulation that may affect value chain and supply chain efficiency. The agencies also often legislate and implement regulation in an uncoordinated manner. That happens because regulators set policies with domestic regulatory objectives in mind. As a consequence, international coordination in these matters is not necessarily able to foster GVCs' production and supply chain trade. Fear that international coordination conflicts with domestic regulatory objectives may explain why existing trade agreements, investment agreements, and similar forms of international cooperation are rarely designed to foster GVC participation (Hoekman 2014).

The G20 and multilateral organizations can help in identifying and lifting the key binding constraints by advocating for a multistakeholder and pragmatic approach to trade policy reform that tackles the so-called deep issues. But efforts are also needed on traditional trade policy issues. In the absence of multilateral reductions in tariffs, low-income countries should seek trade agreements on tariffs, tariff escalation, and standards harmonization with other low-income countries. Previously, low-income countries focused on securing trade agreements with high-income country markets. Today, the trade of intermediate goods in regional and global chains is often between low- and middle-income countries, and emerging economies are becoming important end markets. Import and export tariffs between these countries continue to be relatively high, and these countries are furthermore plagued by a variety of nontariff measures, including quantitative restrictions, technical barriers to trade; and difficulties in allowing harmonization, mutual recognition, and low compliance costs. When these measures restrict trade unnecessarily, simplification and liberalization should be a priority.

Many relevant trade- and investment-related actions to foster participation in GVCs are of a domestic nature. Hence, unilateral action is crucial. Fortunately, most GVC-enhancing reforms will also have a positive impact on non-GVC trade and on overall competitiveness and economic development more generally. But international cooperation matters greatly too, in fact unilateral action and international cooperation are mutually reinforcing each other.

Inclusive Global Value Chains • http://dx.doi.org/10.1596/978-1-4648-0842-5

Advancing cooperation at the international level requires addressing the regional versus the multilateral dimension. Regional trade agreements are important ways to push forward deep integration agendas that are particularly beneficial to SMEs and low- and middle-income countries. The OECD (2012) provides abundant "case story" examples of the importance of regional trading initiatives. For example, in 2006, the Greater Mekong Subregion undertook to enhance trade by constructing bridges and roads in conjunction with its Cross-Border Transport Agreement (CBTA) between the Lao People's Democratic Republic, Thailand, and Vietnam. The CBTA covered nearly all aspects of goods and services flows—including customs inspections, transit traffic, and road and bridge design. As a consequence, average trade value rose by more than 50 percent—to US$142 million in 2006–07, from US$93.5 million in 1999–2000. Average travel times were cut by half along the corridor. Time spent crossing selected borders also fell by 30–50 percent, and the average number of vehicle crossings per day increased. Finally, in June 2009, the CBTA allowed issuance of licenses for some 500 trucks to operate along the corridor without trans-shipment fees.

Brülhart and Hoppe (2012) recount a case where potential regional trade has not yet materialized, precisely because of the absence of CBTA-type collaboration. Kinshasa-Brazzaville is the third-largest urban agglomeration in Africa and is destined to be the largest by 2025. But it has a river border running through it. The Republic of Congo's imports from the Democratic Republic of Congo are a mere 1 percent of the Republic of Congo's total imports, and daily cross-river passenger travel is only 20 percent of the volume of passenger traffic through the Berlin Wall in 1988. The authors calculate that the transit costs would be equivalent to charging Californians commuting from Oakland to San Francisco (about the same distance) between US$1,200 and US$2,400 per trip.

More recent regional trade agreements often contain provisions on government procurement, arrangement of business conditions for investment, or protection of intellectual property rights. They can facilitate closer cooperation and continuous exchange between public officials from the countries involved to reduce barriers to commerce. These provisions often have a higher payoff in trade expansion than that achieved by simply removing tariffs. Jensen and Tarr (2011), using computable general equilibrium prospective analysis, found that mutual reductions in tariffs as part of a comprehensive free trade agreement between Armenia and the European Union would provide some gains for Armenia, but these were dwarfed by actions that would liberalize services, reduce border costs, and harmonize standards. What is critical to emphasize in the present context is that regional trade agreements should serve as a means for achieving deeper integration while continuing to move forward at the multilateral level.

Other important areas of international cooperation include promoting coherence between preferential trade agreements and the WTO, and enabling the GVC participation of low-income countries through Aid for Trade. Priority areas for the latter include financing investment in trade-related infrastructure; reducing standards compliance costs, in particular for SMEs; improving customs operations and border crossings; and enhancing regulatory capacity, particularly in the services sector.

Possible tensions in the international arena are, however, possible. Different interests may arise, as some countries seek to preserve their domestic value added or to enact policies of indigenization. Areas of tension may include tariff escalation policies, subsidies, export restrictions, local content requirements, intellectual property rights, competition policy and regulations on state-owned enterprises, and the level of appropriate standards. Moreover, as GVCs move forward, responding to the push of "next generation" technologies, additional problematic issues may arise. For example, the balance between privacy and data trade opening, rules on intellectual property protection and diffusion of new technologies, or cross-border spillovers of domestic regulations. An example of the latter is provided by the recent French law allowing extraterritoriality in the prosecution of crimes committed by French corporations in their supply chain abroad.

Services Liberalization Agenda
The shift in manufacturing worldwide determined by the increasing dominance of GVCs has been accompanied by important changes in the services sector too, underscoring the importance of the nexus of goods, services, and foreign direct investment (FDI). Services trade and the role of services in boosting the economy as a whole have increased: more than 60 percent of the current stock of global FDI is in services. The composition of services has also changed, with modern services gaining in importance at the expense of traditional services. FDI is also a main engine of growth for services trade. Mode 3 (delivery through foreign affiliates) covers about 50 percent of overall services trade (Saez et al. 2015). Not only has the services trade increased over time, but services have increased their importance as a determinant of competitiveness in the economy as a whole, and SMEs integrate into GVCs predominantly as services providers. Countries with a higher content of services in the downstream economy are also those producing more complex goods (Saez et al. 2015).

The explosion of services and services trade has been caused by falling trade and investment barriers as well as new digital technology, which have reduced costs for service delivery across borders and transformed many goods into services (Taglioni and Winkler 2016). The deregulation in air and road transport, abolition of antitrust exemptions for maritime liner transport, privatization of ports and port services, and divestiture and breakup of telecommunications monopolies are, according to Hoekman (2014), the main examples of regulatory measures that have reduced the cost of service delivery across borders. However, substantial barriers remain in the services sector that act as essential enablers in the geographic dispersion of GVCs. Liberalization of those services that allow for connecting competitively to the world economy and for more efficient access to resources is a priority. Such services include ICT, supply chain management (to reduce inventories, shorten lead times, and enable faster customer response), and improved logistics.

The policy agenda in services should emphasize the relevance of services liberalization for competitiveness in trade and GVCs, as well as focus on regulations and requirements pertaining to areas critical to successful GVC participation, such as the following:

- Cross-border transfer of data and money
- Costs of telecommunications services
- Competitiveness and costs of port and logistics services
- Air transport regulations.

Ensuring That the Benefits of Openness Reach beyond Large Firms and the G20 to SMEs and Low-Income Countries

Many reforms that are essential to raising global welfare will need to take place in some of the world's poorest countries. The G20 ministers' discussion provides an excellent opportunity to consider how trade-related reforms can lead to benefits in economies outside the G20, and how these can trickle down to SMEs at home and in input-supplying countries. Cooperation among the G20 and multilateral organizations can foster and promote several measures.

Quality and Product Certification and Compliance with International Standards

Mutual recognition or convergence of public and private voluntary standards, through national or international guidelines, could help. Upstream firms supplying components to several destinations may no longer incur burdensome certification procedures multiple times for the same product or have to duplicate production processes to comply with conflicting standards. In food value chains, for example, the process standards adapted to one country's requirements may render exporting to another country infeasible. Promoting the convergence of standards and certification requirements and encouraging mutual recognition agreements can go a long way toward alleviating the burden of compliance and enhancing the competitiveness of small-scale exporters. That is true for environmental and social sustainability standards as well as for quality and safety standards.

Improving standards requires much more than simply adopting and enforcing new rules. It requires long-term commitment and incentives and mechanisms tailored to the particular needs of specific countries and specific value chains. The international community should foster or trigger a "race to the top" by developing a common approach for upward graduation through standards implementation. This will require a holistic, country-focused, multistakeholder approach to capacity building that is sustained over time and which will include the following:

- Engagement of the private sector (local suppliers, global leads, and buyers)
- Creation of a local supplier base for advisory services
- Improvement of infrastructure
- Improvements in the business environment.

Acting at those many levels requires the active involvement of many actors:

- *Partnerships.* The G20 could work to strengthen global partnerships with governments, businesses, consumer and labor groups, and international organizations. An inclusive partnership approach opens the door to the best insights and most successful models from those with experience in raising standards, improving productivity, developing skills, and spreading prosperity through participation in GVCs. The Better Work program—a partnership between the World Bank Group's International Finance Corporation and the International Labour Organization—exemplifies how partnerships can make an impact. Further, the G20 could provide support to Business 20 (B20) initiatives geared toward strengthening SMEs' ability to comply with international standards. For example, it would be useful to provide support to set up a multinational enterprise working group within the B20 Trade or SME and Entrepreneurship Task Force, with (a) the objective to elaborate a blueprint on responsible and inclusive GVCs and (b) pledges to provide SMEs the tools and knowledge required for their successful compliance with international standards.

- *G20 countries.* The G20 countries are showing increasing interest in helping low-income countries identify growth and development opportunities that also meet high international standards for goods and services. But it is the knowledge of the G20 countries as much as their financial assistance that can make the difference. Many of their governments have experience to share on how to establish regulatory measures and policies that support higher standards and foster productivity and shared value in GVCs. Being home to many of the world's leading firms, they can enhance the capacity to comply throughout global production chains and thereby help all parties. Being home to the largest consumer markets, they also have a role to play in ensuring transparency and awareness of the challenges faced by SMEs and low-income countries in joining GVCs and leveraging them for economic and social development.

- *Low-income countries.* Increasingly aware of the triple bottom line approach to sustainable growth, many countries have adopted legislation to protect workers and the environment and are working to strengthen the enabling environment. But enforcement offices generally have limited resources; they need the know-how, skills, and capacity to phase in adherence to internationally recognized standards. The process can be self-perpetuating because the likelihood of countries complying with standards increases with greater revenues. Prioritizing the attraction of GVCs whose business models allow greater value-added growth may help by generating the economic space to implement standards.

- *Private sector and civil society.* Leading firms' emphasis on quality and standards represents an important area for potential spillovers in the domestic market. Many of these firms are already providing technical assistance to local suppliers and producers to improve activities along production chains—the business case is strong. But their focus is often on the legal coverage and a narrow gamut of issues. Meanwhile, civil society's advocacy campaigns and technical assistance help mainstream sustainable practices and adherence to international standards. These organizations also help by providing innovative solutions to difficult problems, especially in bringing transparency and in monitoring and evaluating progress. The G20 could help by endorsing initiatives by non-state actors.

Credit Constraints

Although production in GVCs is taking place at the international and often at the global scale, financing economic activity is still largely done at the national scale, and in a fragmented way with little continuity across financial service providers and along the value chain. Moreover, SMEs face specific challenges. Size and intangibility play against their creditworthiness. In general, markets provide less financing than is socially desirable for SMEs that are willing to grow and innovate, and banks routinely rely on balance sheet data, past performance, current turnover, and liquidity as predictors of repayment ability.

Because of these constraints and challenges, policy action may be helpful. This report, for example, highlights the need for financing that takes into account intrinsic know-how, the pool of talent, distribution channels, business relationships, the business model, and access to technology in the valuation of repayment ability. Forms of engaged, patient equity financing and bank guarantees are likely to be preferred to traditional debt financing. Finally, promoting policies that have a multipronged approach may also be helpful. The results from a recent survey carried out by the Italian government seeking to promote the internationalization of SMEs (SIMEST 2012) offer insights as to the needs for overcoming bottlenecks in the financing of GVC participation by SMEs. The ingredients of the approach suggested by the Italian agency SIMES include (a) promoting a policy that has regional connectivity, (b) connecting more than one region together (a low-income region and a non-low-income region), and (c) forming a public-private partnership to fix all the objectives and responsibilities and that defines eligibility criteria, cross-border projects, and sector coverage, entry, and exit.

Dynamic Gains through the Broader Set of Productivity-Enhancing Policies

Although the policies that have been mentioned in this chapter create the necessary framework conditions for SMEs and low-income countries to participate in GVCs, their effects may not be sufficient to ensure that firms in low-income countries will be successful in participating in GVCs. This is because the broad, key challenge for suppliers that want to integrate into GVCs or strengthen and upgrade their participation in GVCs is increasing productivity.

Fostering productivity growth is, however, challenging, and it requires interventions in multiple areas simultaneously to address the internal and external constraints to firm-level efficiency (OECD 2015). These interventions are geared to have a positive impact on the *within* and *between* components of productivity growth. The within component is related to individual firms becoming more productive, that is, increasing the amount of output they produce with a constant amount of input by strengthening their internal capabilities. The between component is associated with the reallocation of factors of production, such as labor and capital, toward more efficient firms, forcing inefficient firms to exit the market and creating the right market conditions for productive firms to thrive. Recent OECD work points to three areas that are particularly important for productivity growth (OECD 2015): (a) fostering innovation at the global frontier and facilitating the diffusion of new technologies to firms at the national frontier; (b) creating a market environment where the most productive firms are allowed to thrive, thereby facilitating the more widespread penetration of available technologies; and (c) reducing resource misallocation, including skill mismatches. Reviving diffusion and improving resource allocation have the potential not only to sustain and accelerate productivity growth, but also to make this growth more inclusive by allowing more firms, notably SMEs, to reap the benefits of the knowledge economy.

Productivity-enhancing policies, which are crucial to make the SMEs involved in GVC activities resilient to external shocks, are frequently part of the national agenda. However, coordinated efforts at the regional level can pay significant rewards, as GVCs are usually a regional phenomenon. A key policy that increases firm productivity is fostering innovation. Given its cross-cutting and systematic nature (OECD 2015), the innovation agenda requires coordinated interventions nationally and regionally, with multiple actors, ministries, and agencies participating in the policy making and implementation of reforms. It also needs organizational and institutional change to be successful (Fagerberg, Srholec, and Verspagen 2009).

Policies oriented toward promoting innovation should focus on building comprehensive innovation ecosystems and operate at different levels: (a) improving framework conditions by, for example, promoting product market competition, strengthening intellectual property rights systems, and financing innovation (including seed and venture capital funds); (b) building innovation capacity and innovation skills by, for example, creating research and technology organizations, quality and technology transfer systems, and training centers; and (c) facilitating connectivity and system articulation by, for example, supporting public-private collaborations for innovation, articulating actors in the technology transfer process, facilitating venture acceleration networks, and promoting the creation of clusters and knowledge spillover effects.[1]

Improving access to digital networks is of particular importance, given its dual role in enhancing productivity and strengthening SMEs' access to global markets. Although considerable progress has been made in strengthening the access of low- and middle-income economies to communications infrastructure, being connected is only the first step (OECD 2013, 2015). A reliable and competitive offer has to be available in markets before the Internet economy can truly take root, which requires policies focused on competition and access. Low- and middle-income economies can benefit from new technological developments, such as mobile and cloud computing, which can help overcome the lack of resources and infrastructure at the domestic level. However, access to cloud resources requires the buildup of domestic infrastructure as well as policy frameworks, for example, to ensure privacy and security. Standardization is also key to the further deployment of cloud services in low- and middle-income economies and low-income countries. Finally, ICT skills adapted to the new dominant technologies have to be developed. These include not only "hard" technical skills, but also "soft" skills and the ability to navigate the complex and ever-growing opportunities, open-source technologies and services, and information available on the global scale.

Given the range of policies that affects innovation across the government, close coordination and appropriate governance mechanisms are essential too, as are monitoring and evaluation to ensure a process for policy improvement and learning over time (OECD 2015).

Further, the productivity agenda should focus on facilitating access to talent at the managerial and workforce levels. SMEs in low-income countries are frequently plagued by weak managerial capacities and inefficient organization. Those weaknesses are reflected in low levels of productivity, suboptimal use of the workforce, waste of materials and inputs, and low efficiency at the level of the production floor. These firms also suffer from the lack of a skilled workforce; thus, they are incapable of conducting simple and complex GVC activities at competitive prices. Policies oriented toward addressing both issues include interventions geared toward improving managerial skills and fostering a long-term entrepreneurial view, increasing the supply of skilled workers in sectors where there is excess demand, and improving workforce skills while reducing skills mismatch. General business education and training programs are the most popular components of entrepreneurship support programs to foster firm productivity. Vocational training, direct financial assistance to local initiatives aimed at fostering work-based learning, facilitation of public-private dialogue to incorporate private sector needs into vocational training and university curricula, and support for the development of sector skills councils that help match firms with employees also contribute to reducing the skills mismatch and enhancing firm productivity.

Finally, the agenda should consider the elimination of economic distortions in factor and product prices, which affect firms' optimal input choices and end up facilitating the survival of large and inefficient firms. These distortions, which reflect heterogeneous policy treatment of firms within a sector, create significant dispersion of firm performance, even within very narrowly defined sectors. Firm productivity dispersion, a measure of allocative inefficiency, negatively affects aggregate productivity at the sector and economy levels, diminishing the impact of productivity-enhancing policies—such as those aimed at fostering product market competition to ignite innovation or promoting exports through the reduction of fixed costs—when these policies target the average firm.

Investing in Expanding the Statistical Basis and Technical Analysis of Participation in GVCs

A significant, and often overlooked, way to facilitate successful integration into GVCs, particularly for low-income countries, includes (a) correctly identifying constraints and remedial actions and (b) assessing the efficacy of new policy measures. This cuts across the gamut of the statistical information system, including macro and, crucially, micro (firm-level) data. The OECD-WTO Trade in Value Added (TiVA) database is one of the well-known recent examples of statistical initiatives to provide country- and sector-level evidence for supporting GVC analysis. Although the database currently includes 61 economies, few low-income countries, particularly in Africa and Central Asia, are included.

Significant efforts are needed to develop and improve the national building blocks required for inclusion in the TiVA database. Needed improvements include national supply-use and input-output tables of better quality, as well as more granularity for trade-in-services data, developed in line with international accounting standards—the System of National Accounts and the *Balance of Payments and International Investment Position Manual.* Other standard macro-level data collection areas where further investment would be beneficial include structural business statistics, trade-by-enterprise characteristics, entrepreneurship indicators (business demography), and foreign affiliate trade statistics.

All of these standard collections require good data at the firm level. Investment in and scaling up of microdata and existing data collections and surveys are central priorities for better policy making. The World Bank Group Enterprise Surveys use standard survey instruments to collect firm-level data on the business environment from business owners and top managers. The surveys account for firm size and cover a broad range of topics, including access to finance, corruption, infrastructure, crime, competition, labor, obstacles to growth, and performance measures, but not yet participation in GVCs. Other available data sets include microenterprise, informal, sector-specific, and other surveys. Panel (longitudinal) data sets of survey results are available for many countries.

These statistics constitute an excellent basis for expanding the available tools for better documentation of the business relationships taking place in the context of GVCs. This includes collecting firm-level information on the links between exporters and foreign buyers and between local firms and multinational companies integrated in GVCs (backward and forward linkages), as well as information on the internal and external factors facilitating or impeding accession and upgrading of firms in GVCs. The nature of participation in GVCs by firms in low-income countries and of different behaviors by large and small firms in the adoption of international certification practices and regulatory standards or in the use of ICT and other technology are among the areas that could be better documented through embedding a GVC module in the existing Enterprise Surveys. Impact evaluations of policy interventions that can facilitate access to and upgrading of participation in GVCs by SMEs and firms in low-income countries are also necessary to help prioritize interventions, strengthen the evidence base for policy making, and coordinate actions among actors, often from different countries.

Box 4.1 summarizes the key take-away messages from this chapter.

Box 4.1 Key Take-Away Messages from Chapter 4

- The determinants of success in international markets range from productive capacity to infrastructure and services, the business environment, the assurance of efficient trade and investment flows, and good connectivity overall. Thus, there is broad scope for policy initiatives that can be helpful in addressing the challenges that low-income countries face in integrating into global value chains (GVCs).
- Human capital problems, including weak organization of production, can be addressed by policies that combine high-quality initial education with lifelong learning opportunities for all, to help ensure that workers are well prepared for the future. Other useful approaches include (a) developing and implementing global platforms for sharing best practices and e-learning, with attention to vocational training and all functions (including sales, market-ing, and knowledge of languages); (b) leveraging buyers to train local staff as an efficient means of knowledge transfer; (c) harnessing informal entrepreneurship, particularly the informal businesses that seem to prevail in the downstream parts of GVCs; and (d) reducing skills mismatch and facilitating resource allocation across the economy.
- Innovation and technology adoption involves product innovation, process and organiza-tional change, and even marketing and branding strategies. With small and medium enterprises (SMEs) facing the most severe challenges, policies should include several com-plementary elements, including (a) developing and implementing rigorous intellectual property legislation, (b) providing assistance to SMEs and firms in low-income countries through electronic platforms that help domestic firms acquire foreign technology and com-mercialize their intellectual property, and (c) assisting SMEs in using freely available tech-nologies or acquiring technological licensing agreements. Strengthening collaboration with universities and multinational firms can also enhance access to knowledge and technology.
- Trade and trade-related policies remain important, as GVCs magnify the cost of protectionist measures and trade costs fall disproportionately on SMEs. Reordering priorities in trade policy—giving as much consideration to imports, upstream services, and timeliness as to exports and market access—is important. This includes prioritizing import tariff stream-lining and simplifying export procedures to ensure a more level playing field for SMEs. The swift and effective ratification and implementation of the World Trade Organization's Trade Facilitation Agreement and the improvement of services sector efficiencies are key priorities. It is important to design reforms as coherent packages of hard and soft infrastruc-ture for domestic and international initiatives.
- Efficient logistics are important, with the costs for SMEs estimated to be double the costs for large companies, and structural difficulties for SMEs in remote areas of low-income countries

box continues next page

Box 4.1 Key Take-Away Messages from Chapter 4 *(continued)*

in serving global markets with high-value products, such as fresh agri-produce. Effective approaches require assisting countries in designing and implementing customized solutions that are able to meet specific needs, operational circumstances, and national connectivity priorities. Effective approaches also require providing a continuum of potential support activities, including logistics performance assessments, development of practical implementation plans, and identification of sources of financing for implementation plans. Domestic initiatives need to be matched with supporting initiatives in transit and destination markets to be effective, as some successful experiences in Latin America have shown. Hence international cooperation and dialogue are important in guiding effective reform of the logistics system and global physical connectivity.

- Beyond physical connectivity, information and communication technology (ICT) connectivity is also important and requires investment in infrastructure and policies to ensure access at competitive prices. Services sector efficiency improvements and collective efforts to establish global online platforms and to facilitate the access of SMEs and low-income countries to ICT networks would go a long way in (a) helping those firms internationalize; (b) fostering the emergence of "micro-multinationals" (that is, small and young firms that are global from their inception); and (c) leveraging ICT.

- With increased public and private focus on certification of quality and products and standards for the sustainable management of GVCs, but high costs of compliance for SMEs, there is a large role to be played by collective action. Mutual recognition and convergence of dominant private and public standards would reduce the costs and burden of certification and compliance for SMEs and firms in low-income countries. Moreover, a holistic, country-focused, multistakeholder approach to capacity building that is sustained over time is necessary. Global platforms for sharing best practices and learning are likely to be useful instruments for identifying solutions that maximize productivity and economic growth while supporting certification and compliance with standards.

- In general, markets provide less than the socially desirable amount of financing for SMEs that are willing to grow and innovate because of their smaller size and greater intangibility. Therefore, innovative financial instruments are necessary to encourage young and innovative SMEs and firms in low-income countries to participate in GVCs. Financing that takes into account intrinsic know-how, the pool of talent, distribution channels, business relationships, the business model, and access to technology in valuation of repayment ability is important. Forms of equity financing and bank guarantees are likely to be better adapted to the needs of SME and low-income country suppliers to GVCs than traditional debt financing based on balance sheet data, past performance, current turnover, and liquidity as predictors of repayment ability. Promoting policies that include regional connectivity between low-income countries and non-low-income countries, public-private partnerships and engagement, creation of a private market for financial services provision, cross-border projects, and sector coverage is likely to help.

- Finally, a significant, and often overlooked, barrier to successful integration in GVCs, particularly in low-income countries, is poor statistical capacity, which prevents the correct identification of constraints, remedial actions, and their impact. Investment in better statistics across the gamut of the statistical information system, including macro and, crucially, micro (firm-level) data, is desirable.

Note

1. A successful example of a regional initiative oriented toward fostering business innovation is the Western Balkans Enterprise Development and Innovation Facility, which is funded by the European Union and implemented in cooperation with the World Bank Group, OECD, European Bank for Reconstruction and Development, and European Investment Bank, with the purpose of improving access to finance for innovative SMEs in the region.

References

Brülhart, Marius, and Mombert Hoppe. 2012. "Economic Integration in the Lower Congo Region: Opening the Kinshasa–Brazzaville Bottleneck." In *De-Fragmenting Africa: Deepening Regional Trade Integration in Goods and Services*, edited by Paul Brenton and Gözde Isik, 33–41. Washington, DC: World Bank.

Fagerberg, Jan, Martin Srholec, and Bart Verspagen. 2009. "Innovation and Economic Development." MERIT Working Paper 032, United Nations University—Maastricht Economic and Social Research Institute on Innovation and Technology (MERIT), Maastricht, Netherlands.

Hoekman, Bernard. 2014. *Supply Chains, Mega-Regionals, and the WTO.* Washington, DC: Center for Economic Policy Research.

Jensen, Jesper, and David G. Tarr. 2011. "Deep Trade Policy Options for Armenia: The Importance of Trade Facilitation, Services and Standards Liberalization." *Economics: The Open Access E-Journal* 6 (1): 1–54.

OECD (Organisation for Economic Co-operation and Development). 2012. "A Survey of Policy Makers for the OECD Project on Fostering Small and Medium-Sized Participation in Global Markets." OECD Centre for SMEs, Entrepreneurship and Local Development, Paris.

———. 2013. *Supporting Investment in Knowledge Capital, Growth and Innovation.* Paris: OECD Publishing.

———. 2015. *The Future of Productivity.* Paris: OECD Publishing.

OECD, WTO, and UNCTAD (Organisation for Economic Co-operation and Development, World Trade Organization, and United Nations Conference on Trade and Development). 2013. *Implications of Global Value Chains for Trade, Investment, Development, and Jobs.* Report prepared for the G20 Leaders Summit, St. Petersburg, Russian Federation, September 5–6. http://www.oecd.org/sti/ind/G20-Global-Value-Chains-2013.pdf.

OECD (Organisation for Economic Co-operation and Development), WTO (World Trade Organization), and World Bank. 2014. *Global Value Chains: Challenges, Opportunities, and Implications for Policy.* Report prepared for the G20 Trade Ministers Meeting, Sydney, July 19.

Saez, Sebastian, Daria Taglioni, Erik van der Marel, Claire H. Hollweg, and Veronika Zavacka. 2015. *Valuing Services in Trade: A Toolkit for Competitiveness Diagnostics.* Washington, DC: World Bank.

SIMEST (Società italiana per le imprese all'estero). 2012. "The Mediterranean Partnership Fund." Unpublished manuscript, SIMEST, Rome.

Taglioni, Daria and Deborah Winkler. 2016. "Making Global Value Chains Work for Development." World Bank, Washington, DC.

Environmental Benefits Statement

The World Bank Group is committed to reducing its environmental footprint. In support of this commitment, the Publishing and Knowledge Division leverages electronic publishing options and print-on-demand technology, which is located in regional hubs worldwide. Together, these initiatives enable print runs to be lowered and shipping distances decreased, resulting in reduced paper consumption, chemical use, greenhouse gas emissions, and waste.

The Publishing and Knowledge Division follows the recommended standards for paper use set by the Green Press Initiative. The majority of our books are printed on Forest Stewardship Council (FSC)–certified paper, with nearly all containing 50–100 percent recycled content. The recycled fiber in our book paper is either unbleached or bleached using totally chlorine-free (TCF), processed chlorine-free (PCF), or enhanced elemental chlorine-free (EECF) processes.

More information about the Bank's environmental philosophy can be found at http://www.worldbank.org/corporateresponsibility.

green
press
INITIATIVE

www.ingramcontent.com/pod-product-compliance
Lightning Source LLC
Chambersburg PA
CBHW080426270326
41929CB00018B/3172